MW00637896

BEYOND DRAMA

TRANSCENDING ENERGY VAMPIRES

by

Nate Regier, PhD and Jeff King, LMSW

Next Element Publishing

Newton, Kansas

2013

 next element

Next Element Publishing
414 North Main, Suite 200
Newton, KS 67114
316-283-4200
www.next-element.com

BEYOND DRAMA: TRANSCENDING ENERGY VAMPIRES
© 2013 by Next Element Consulting, LLC

All rights reserved. No part of this book may be used or reproduced in any manner whatsoever without permission in writing from the publisher, except in the case of brief quotations embodied in critical articles or reviews.

Library of Congress Cataloging-in-Publication Data

Next Element Consulting, LLC, 2013
Beyond Drama: Transcending Energy Vampires / Nate Regier and Jeff King
Includes bibliographical references
ISBN: 978-0-9860535-0-4 (paperback)

Cover and interior design: Flint Hills Design, North Newton, KS

Printed in the United States of America

OVERVIEW

Drama is what happens when people struggle against themselves or others to feel justified about the things they do to gain negative attention, with or without awareness. Drama is an energy vampire, sucking the lifeblood out of everyone and everything around it. Drama strains relationships, sidelines teams, and causes companies to operate at a fraction of their capacity. Drama is amazingly predictable yet incredibly resistant to change.

Why does drama happen, why do you allow it, and how can you change it? *Beyond Drama* answers these questions, providing a guide to understand how drama plays out in your life and how to transform it into compassionate accountability, professionally and personally.

The word *Compassion* originates from the Latin root meaning "to struggle with," a profound step beyond just getting along. To help you achieve com-passionate accountability, *Beyond Drama* will challenge you with provocative new approaches to tough issues, such as responsibility, accountability, expectations, humility, and the Golden Rule.

Whether you use this book to improve family relationships, as a team-build-ing exercise, or as required reading for your executive team, *Beyond Drama* is your guide to achieve greater awareness, effectiveness, and accountability in everything you do.

FORWARD

Nate Regier and Jeff King's *Beyond Drama: Transcending Energy Vampires* is indeed a journey of how for the Process Age. Their book is a practical and applicable guide to increasing our possibilities for professional prosperity as well as enhancing our personal well-being.

For many of us, a GPS (Global Positioning System) helps us get where we want to go on a map. To help us go further in life, Nate and Jeff have given us our own IPS — Individual Positioning System, which identifies where we are with ourselves and others, how to keep ourselves on track, how to deal with the detours, speed bumps, and potholes, and how to keep our energies up and our needs met in order to reach our goals.

This book is full of invitations and examples of how to realize that the very corners of distress we find ourselves in can very well be personal and professional growth opportunities.

When Yogi Berra gave guests directions to his home, he often finished with, "and when you come to the fork in the road, take it."

Yogi lived on a cul-de-sac.

Jeff and Nate, thanks for this gift you have prepared so wisely for the reader. Your information provides new views of our life's journey, and inspiring us to appreciate the joys along the way.

– Taibi Kahler, President of Kahler Communications Inc.

ACKNOWLEDGEMENTS

I've heard from other authors that the first book is the most difficult. I don't know if this is true — yet. I do know that without my terrific team at Next Element, this project would have never made it beyond the conceptual stage. Thank you for giving me permission and encouragement to put our collective experience into the pages of this book, letting me have space to do the work on my terms, and holding me accountable when other shiny objects competed for my attention. Above all, thank you for practicing what you preach everyday.

I want to give special thanks to Norm's Coffee Bar in my hometown of Newton, Kansas. Norm's is my haven, my favorite place to write. Robert, you make the best French press in the world! Our first book signing will be at Norm's, and the first one is on me!

To all the people in my stories and case studies, named or unnamed, thank you! You have been the fabric of my life, the context within which I have struggled, learned, grown, and found my true passion.

Steven Karpman and Taibi Kahler, your discoveries have changed my life. I appreciate your brilliance, creativity, curiosity, encouragement, and perspective. You have helped me understand what it means to own my potency.

Julie, my fabulous wife, you are my inspiration to pursue drama-free living everyday. Life with you and our three daughters gives me more joy and purpose than I ever thought possible. Thank you for your support, encouragement, and belief in me throughout this journey.

Jeff King, my coauthor, business partner, friend, and sparring buddy: You keep me laughing. You keep me on my toes. And you keep me honest. I am grateful for the creativity and energy you've brought into my life and to this book.

– Nate Regier

I want to first thank a man by the name of Paul Unruh. He was the first mentor in my life and the person who introduced me to the concept of "change your language change your life." Paul, thank you for being a mentor and a role model.

Big thanks to Nate, Jamie, and Michele. In 2008 when we all formed Next Element, it was a first for all us and a scary first step that has paid off tenfold. The three of you are inspirations!

To my coauthor and friend Nate. Thank you! Writing this book has been a first for us and we have accomplished the intention that we set out for ourselves. I will always remember the Arbuckle mountains, where we starting constructing and writing, when we were not cooking wings or exploring the mountains.

To my wife, Rebecca Amis, thank you so much for supporting me and believing in me. This book is only possible because you believed in me and said YES to all my crazy ideas. I cannot express in words how much of an inspiration you are to me. Thank you for being you!

Maggie and Harper, thank you for being in my world!

Derrien, thanks for being authentic to who you are and uncompromising on the person who you want to be in this world. You have taught me to be a better person. Thank you.

– Jeff King

CONTENTS

The Problem
▼

▲
The Solution

The Toolkit

INTRODUCTION

Drama is an energy vampire, sucking the lifeblood out of everyone and everything around it. Drama strains relationships, sidelines teams, and causes companies to operate at a fraction of their capacity. Enterprises that allow drama to dominate don't survive for long. Ones that build cultures free of drama can thrive.

What do we mean by "drama"? Drama is what happens when people under stress or distress try to justify their actions even when it hurts themselves or their relationships. Our goal in this book is to help you understand the drama that may be playing out in your own work or home life and how to transform it into conscious, compassionate collaboration.

Our company, Next Element, opened for business on October 13, 2008. Many will remember this month as the official start of the recession. It wasn't our plan to start a business in a recession. And, everyday we thank our lucky stars for this wonderful twist of fate. Next Element is a professional training and consulting firm specializing in reducing drama and increasing compassion in corporate and personal relationships. Drama is expensive, wasteful, and time-consuming. Ironically, most companies spend all their efforts streamlining systems and procedures while avoiding the elephant in the room — interpersonal drama.

Many predicted that we'd never make it past our first year. Entering our fifth year, Next Element has thrived and we are growing! In 2013 we were honored to be selected as a top-five finalist for small business of the year by the Wichita Kansas Metro Area Chamber of Commerce.

How have we been successful? We've focused on practicing what we preach — building a drama-free culture inside our own company. Our toolkit is all about transcending drama, and pursuing compassionate contribution. And, it starts with us. Living this philosophy in every interaction is a full-time responsibility. In the way we run staff meetings, how we conduct ourselves at networking events, and how we build relationships with our clients and our families, eliminating drama is our goal. It is the foundation upon which everything else rests.

We didn't have MBAs. We didn't have entrepreneurial experience. We had zero startup capital and haven't borrowed a dime. We knew we could learn about business plans, product lines, accounting, strategic goals, social media, and sales. And the one thing that tied us together was the belief that no aspect of our operational life could be ultimately successful unless we kept drama at bay. Has it been easy? No. It's been the hardest thing any of us has ever done. Drama is human nature. The more passionate you are, the more it wants in. Transcending drama requires constant vigilance, a willingness to engage in productive conflict with each other, and openness to daily growth. Operating a company with a no-drama culture is the most thrilling, liberating, and energizing experience we've ever had. Our passion is to help others experience it, too.

Beyond Drama is a roadmap to transcend drama in your life. This book is a highly practical deep-dive into personal and professional effectiveness. From understanding the dynamics behind organizational and global conflict to decoding power struggles between you and your children, we offer readers an insightful and achievable journey towards becoming a better leader, teacher, spouse, parent, mentor, and friend.

We've distilled current best practices in the social sciences, leadership, and communication literature and then sprinkled it with plenty of personal stories, anecdotes, and case studies to keep it real. The tools in this book are not ivory-tower theory. They are down-to-earth, practical steps you can take today to transform relationships. Is this a personal self-help book or a leadership book? Both. Is the focus personal or professional? Again, the answer is both. Drama has no boundaries. Personal drama creeps into our professional lives — and the other way around. Maybe you are a leader in your company. You are probably also a friend, spouse, parent, board member, or coach. Compartmentalizing your life might be possible with regard to specific job duties. Beyond that, such boundaries are meaningless. Our needs, thoughts, and behaviors are all connected.

In an age of too much "what," this book is about the "how." It's about how to become response-able, capable, and confident in building more empowering and fulfilling relationships in every aspect of your life. You can use it effectively as a self-help guide, a book study for your executive team, a resource for becoming a better supervisor, or a discussion starter between you and your life partner.

We've divided the journey into three sections: The Problem, The Solution, and The Toolkit. Section 1, The Problem, outlines what we are all up against. In Chapter 1, "It's Not What You Say, But How You Say It," we demonstrate that the process of how we go about things is often more important than the content of our words and actions. In Chapter 2, "Why Should We Care About Process"? we offer three compelling reasons why a book with this focus is so important right now, as we enter a new era that we call "The Process Age." Chapter 3, "Understanding the Drama Triangle," lays out the basics of negative drama — what it is, why it happens, its impact on you and others, and the key myths that keep it going. Chapter 4, "Drama: A Self-Fulfilling Prophecy," shows how in drama we get exactly what's coming to us, and challenges us to think differently about personal responsibility. Section 1 ends by outlining four important choices we have when faced with drama.

Section 2, The Solution, offers our roadmap for taming and transcending energy vampires in your personal and professional life. This section will challenge assumptions, habits, and what you think you know about being effective. Our goal is to take you beyond your comfort zone and inspire you to be more intentional about eliminating drama from your life. Chapter 5, "A Compassionate Alternative to Drama," gives a whole new meaning to the term "compassion" by describing three core skillsets you can develop to build your drama resistance and begin struggling with people instead of against them.

Chapters 6 and 7 are designed to raise awareness about what drama looks like, sounds like, and feels like. We've discovered nine dimensions of drama, each with signature attitudes, beliefs, and behaviors. Each dimension includes complementary, healthy alternatives. Chapter 6, "Dimensions of Drama: The Big Three," starts with what we believe are the three primary dimensions of drama, and Chapter 7, "Dimensions of Drama: The Rest of the Story," explores six additional dimensions. We invite you to use the drama dimension checklists in these chapters to assess where you currently are and begin framing the conversation about where you want to go in your professional and personal relationships. We encourage you to take the time and energy necessary to do an honest self-assessment and engage in candid discussion with trusted others about what you learn. Take it to the next level with your team or organization by accessing our online Drama Assessment at drama.next-element.com. Change begins with awareness. In Chapter 8, "May I Have Your Attention, Please?" we unveil the "secret recipe" to invite people out of drama and into the arena of effective, compassionate behavior.

Section 3, The Toolkit, offers an array of strategies and disciplines for putting solutions into practice. Chapter 9, "Becoming an Effective Motivator," is a step-by-step guide to applying the information from Chapter 8, along with quick detour into the dark side — what happens when people don't get their psychological needs met? In Chapter 10, "Expectations: The Double-Edged Sword," we take on the tough topics of guilt, shame, and entitlement and show how eliminating expectations can help us to lead more effectively with compassion.

How do we deal with change in the Process Age? Chapter 11, "Change and Drama" and Chapter 12, "Change and Compassion: Transcend and Include," offer an elegant and practical framework for understanding change by looking first at the damaging consequences of drama-based responses to change and then the exciting possibilities that emerge when change is negotiated using the key skills of compassion. Chapter 11 includes change assessments that will help you find out where you are now, accompanied by recommended next steps and leadership responsibilities and opportunities.

How bad do you want it? If moving out of drama and into compassion is your goal, Chapters 13 – 15 will get you started. Drama is a self-fulfilling prophecy and so is compassion. In Chapter 13, "From Attention to Intention," we provide you with five keys to maximizing the laws of attraction in compassion. Chapter 14, "Advocates and Adversaries: Building Healthy Community," explores how profoundly we are defined by our relationships and associations. We look specifically at what adversarial relationships look like in business and personal life and suggest a variety of effective responses to them. In Chapter 15, "The Power of Invitation," we share a tool that is a staple in our own team and in our work with clients — The Formula for Compassionate Conflict. This template and the accompanying examples will help you stay out of drama and invite others to join you in compassionate collaboration.

Chapter 16, "Becoming Self-ful," is all about you, how you are taking care of yourself, and where you are in relation to others in your life. We offer our perspective on self-care and stewardship of your precious spiritual, emotional, mental, psychological, and physical resources.

With awareness comes responsibility. With new learning comes possibility. Are you ready to accept the challenge of response-ability? In Chapter 17, "Living Beyond Drama: Transcending Energy Vampires," we invite you to accept five core challenges necessary to turn what you've learned so far into a powerful force for effectiveness in all aspects of your life.

We invite you to digest *Beyond Drama* at your own pace. Reflect on it in your own space, or share your insights with a trusted friend. As a book study, we guarantee the discussion will be lively. As a personal self-help guide, we believe that you'll be challenged and stimulated to grow. Either way, the roadmap is ready.

Will you accompany us on the journey?

The Problem

CHAPTER 1

It's Not What You Say, But How You Say It

One person says, *"Honey, where would you like to eat dinner tonight?"*
The other responds. *"Oh, I don't care, wherever you want?"*

Now what? Almost anything you do from here forward makes things worse. You know because you've been through this scenario a thousand times. The trouble has nothing to do with what was said, and everything to do with how it was delivered.

The process (method of delivery) carries as much, if not more, weight than the content of what is being communicated. How many times have you attempted to deliver a heartfelt message about which you were passionate and it fell on deaf ears. Worse yet, you got a negative response. This can be the beginning of drama — spending energy trying to justify the content of your message without recognizing that the problem lies in the process.

Substance vs. Style

In his book, *Don't Be Such A Scientist*, our friend, author and filmmaker Randy Olson tells a story of a exercise he did as a student in film school. The students were shown two corporate training videos on how to run a drilling machine in a manufacturing company.

The first video showed a man standing next to the machine, showing all the parts, how they work and explaining in detail how to operate the machine. The camera never moved away from the man and the machine.

In the second video, the camera moved all around the machine, zooming in and out, with romantic lighting, narrated by a seductive female voice. The second video, by design, did not include enough information to effectively explain how to operate the drilling machine.

After viewing the two videos, the class was asked to vote on which video was most effective in getting the message across. The winner — you guessed it — the second video. The class voted style (process) over substance (content).

This exercise illustrates that style is a powerful medium through which substance gets delivered. In the group of film students, compelling packaging led them to believe that the second video's message was more thorough and effective than the video containing complete instructions. Now, the scientists out there may ask the next question: Isn't the proof in the pudding? Preferences on a survey are one thing, but which video would result in better outcomes, better job performance actually operating the drilling machine in real life? Isn't behavior and performance the true test of effectiveness?

Great question! Let's go a little deeper into the substance vs. style issue.

Policies and the Confusion Between Process and Content

During a leadership program we were facilitating, a bank executive shared this story with us. One of the bank's tellers, we'll call her

Suzie, had piercings and tattoos, and never could quite follow the dress code policy. Suzie was given feedback, put on corrective actions plans and was on the brink of termination. In fact, there had even been several executive meetings to revamp the dress code policy so that the guidelines were less ambiguous, hoping that would fix the problem.

And then someone made an observation. Suzie was always on time to work, completed tasks as assigned, and the quality of her work was exemplary. "How do we make sense of this?" wondered one bank executive. "We have dress code policies for a reason and if someone can't follow the policies, how can they be a good employee?" So the bank did what most companies do when they need answers. They conducted a survey. The bank polled customers with whom Suzie interacted on a daily basis. Reasoned the bank executive, "This survey should prove that customers appreciate appropriate attire and justify the importance of our dress code policy. And, our customers will be impressed by our strictly enforced standards."

Guess what happened? The customer survey came back with glowing remarks about Suzie. They loved the employee and raved about how great a worker she was. Specific comments included adjectives such as "friendly," "outgoing," and "willing to help."

Impossible! Surely something was wrong with the survey. How could the bank's carefully considered dress policy be so relatively unimportant to customers? How could a company for whom customer service is so important miss this?

The answer is simple. The way in which Suzie presented herself was not to the liking of bank leadership. A process (style) clash with administration trumped the content (substance) of her exceptional performance. Leadership was unable to see what was important because they were seeking to feel justified. We see this dynamic in every company with which we've worked. Policies that are designed and enforced without awareness of the importance of both process and content lead to countless power struggles, wasted time, and bureaucratic hullabaloo. Aren't policies supposed to encourage and support performance? Aren't they supposed to help us all be more effective at executing the mission of the organization?

Don't get us wrong. We aren't against policies, even dress code guidelines. What we are suggesting is that policies, like the words on this page, are the content. And, they exist and are lived out within contexts. Organizations and individuals can be more effective and experience less conflict when they can distinguish process from content while recognizing that both are necessary. How many policies does your organization have that were written in reaction to the behavior of a small number of people? How many times have you revised your policies, believing that making them stricter or clearer would fix the behavior? How much time have you spent in executive session fussing over a policy that you've rehashed several times? Our informal research has shown a positive correlation between the size and detail of the policy manual and the level of drama in a company. Is writing, refining, and enforcing policies an energy vampire for you?

This book is about recognizing the difference between process and content, negotiating this balance with more skill, and unlocking new energy and inspiration along the way. When process and content work in harmony (as we will show in later in the book), greater levels of effectiveness can be achieved. When content becomes the exclusive focus, self-justification is the prime motivator and drama runs rampant.

Drama can result from an overfocus on content at the expense of process. Several years ago, I (Jeff) worked at a hospital as a psychotherapist and organizational consultant. I was charged with generating 27 hours of billable work each week.

In my final year with the agency, I averaged about 20 billable hours per week and was regularly encouraged by my supervisors to improve my performance. On at least one occasion, I was threatened with a reduction in pay and benefits, per the policy, if I did not improve my performance. Sensing something was not right, I did some research. I discovered that the actual revenue I brought in for the organization that year was approximately $25,000 above the average among my peers who met their billable norm.

I was pretty excited about my discovery, and asked for a meeting with the top administrators. I did my best to explain the data I had gathered from our billing department, and explained how the data (content), of my performance was that I generated more money for the agency than most therapists who made their 27-hour billable hour quota. What I discovered was that by billing less hours (content) I was able to focus on how (process) to bill higher net dollars per hour of services. Sounded like a win-win to me! I also suggested that maybe shifting some of our focus from content (hours billed) to the process of how each employee generates income could help the agency. A small part of me even hoped to be asked to chair a task force that would look into the issue.

I was feeling pretty good about myself and thought maybe my discovery could help out a company struggling to cope with decreasing insurance reimbursement rates and shifting payer mixes. At the very least, I'd be pardoned for my substandard billable norm.

After my presentation one executive looked at me quizzically and asked: "So, Jeff, what do you want from us?" The Vice President added, "Jeff, it is really about the billable norm and there are consequences for not making the norm." Taking one last desperate swing in a fight that I knew I had already lost, I asked. "Are you saying you would rather I make less money as long as I comply with the billable norm?" There were nods all around.

That was the day I knew it was time to go. It was time to begin a journey of helping others discern the difference between content and process, to begin working on drama-free living. As we will show later in the book, one of the signature symptoms focusing too much on content is that people seek to feel justified instead of being effective. It would have been effective to support creative solutions to get more revenue and better results with less time investment. It was justified to enforce a policy and "be right" even in the face of contradictory evidence.

This story is played out in many businesses. And, it's not a new story. This story is as old as policies or profit and loss statements. And, we've begun to understand that the failure to distinguish process from content is responsible for countless business failures, relationship failures, and failures to thrive.

The Power of Process

Process has no conscience. It has no values. It has no sense of right and wrong. It is one of the most powerful forces of human nature. Process precedes and can trump content, no matter how logical, important, and meaningful that message may be. And because process is the vehicle within which the story of our lives unfolds, we can't live without it.

While we were writing this book, Jim Cameron's movie, *Avatar*, broke all box office records for sales. It generated over $1 billion worldwide in its first three weeks. The story of *Avatar* is nothing new. As one reviewer put it, the story is a mishmash of many of the best movie scripts of all time, from *The Wizard of Oz* to *Dances with Wolves*. So how did it become the highest- grossing movie of all time? Not because of the story itself (content), but because of how the story was told (process) and the context in which it exists. There were game-changing special effects, next-generation 3–D filming, and a stunning buffet of visual elements. Substance didn't stand a chance against style in Cameron's hands.

Critics have argued that *Avatar* made a bigger impact on environmental awareness than any movie to date, including Al Gore's *An Inconvenient Truth*. Gore's film, straightforwardly-presented, well-researched, and fact-heavy, is a classic example of how substance alone can go only so far without style to carry it.

CHAPTER 2

Why Should We Care about Process?

Process is important. It can save our day or kick our butts. It can obscure our best intentions, or inspire others to act on our messages. We offer three reasons to take the concept of process seriously.

Process is the Foundation of Social–Emotional Intelligence

Process skills are the core competencies of social-emotional intelligence. Social–emotional intelligence involves the awareness of one's own and others' emotional states, managing these in healthy ways, and using this information to negotiate relationships more effectively. Key components of social-emotional intelligence include self-awareness, other-awareness, self-management, and relationship-management.

In the last 20 years there has been enormous progress in understanding the nature and value of playing nice in the sandbox, both with ourselves and with each other. Being able to effectively negotiate the social and emotional landscape of our lives is hugely important to both well-being and business success. Daniel Goleman has brought emotional intelligence (EQ) to the public eye with several best-selling books.[1] A decade of our personal experience working with companies seeking to develop leadership, morale, and engagement continues to reinforce the power of process behind each of these drivers of success.

Social-emotional intelligence has gained prominence because researchers, business leaders, educators, and parents are increasingly aware that it takes more than intellect to be successful in our changing world. It is well known that standardized tests of book smarts and traditional intelligence tests don't predict success in contemporary life. Knowledge is content. It is helpful and important yet not sufficient to be successful and effective. Social-emotional intelligence is the process, the vehicle by which knowledge becomes performance.

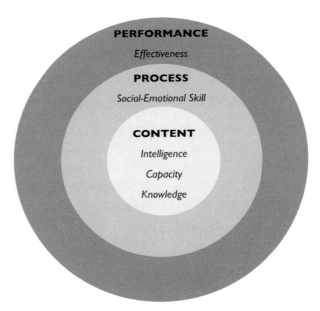

Figure 1. The Relationship Between Content, Process, and Performance

---

1 Emotional Intelligence: Why It Can Matter More than IQ, Random House, 2006; Social Intelligence: The New Science of Human Relationships. Bantam, 2007; Primal Leadership: Learning to Lead with Emotional Intelligence, Harvard Business Review Press, 2004..

Figure 1 shows how we conceptualize the relationship between content, process, and performance. In this illustration, consider content as intelligence, capacity, knowledge — your potential. Performance is the execution of that potential under real-life conditions. These conditions may include stress, unpredictability, boundaries, relationships, the impact of your life experiences, and many other things you cannot control. Capacity and potential do not guarantee performance when it matters. I (Nate) was made painfully aware of this many times growing up when my parents, teachers, and coaches told me that I wasn't living up to my potential. What they were saying is "you have the capacity to perform much better, to make a more significant impact than you're now making."

What predicts whether potential will become real-life performance? It turns out that it's all about social-emotional competencies. There is plenty of research showing that these skills strongly predict and determine how potential becomes performance. The majority of leaders we work with would choose a less skilled but highly social-emotionally competent employee over a person with great technical skills and little ability to operate within relationships. All social-emotional competencies are process skills.

We recently partnered with a large multi-specialty medical provider in a two-year project to transform their outpatient family practice clinics into Patient Centered Medical Homes (PCMH) that met the highest quality and performance standards. Our role was to support their team-alignment and communication skills components. In reviewing the research on PCMH initiatives nationwide, a consistent theme emerged. Those who successfully made the transition from traditional care models to a PCMH model had one thing in common — aligned, supportive teams who understood the difference between content and process. Changing practice habits, learning new records systems, transforming patient flow are difficult and stressful content adjustments. This "what" could only be accomplished when the "how" of teamwork, support, mutual respect and open communication were present.

This leads us to the second reason why process skills are critical for transforming drama into compassionate contribution.

The Stakes Are High

Failure to pay attention to process has more dire consequences than ever before. The reason is not because process is more important than it used to be. It's because content is more potent than it used to be. The stakes are higher than they have ever been. As humans, we now have the capacity to destroy ourselves and render our earth uninhabitable for humans. We also have the capacity to solve huge problems such as poverty, disease, and environmental degradation.

Coupled with this powerful capacity to both destroy and create is an unprecedented flow of information. We live in a global community, connected in multiple ways, communicating in realtime around the world. It is possible to know instantly what is happening anywhere, anytime. Governments can no longer keep their actions secret because of mobile communication devices and the Internet. The best-kept company secret could be posted on YouTube and go viral by this afternoon. Google has the capacity to follow your every move and recommend the perfect restaurant based on your diet, what time of day it is, and where you are. You can track the exact location of your teenage daughter using the GPS on her smart phone, and receive regular text updates if you wish.

How does all of this capacity and all this connectedness get translated into something meaningful, useful, effective, and productive? Process. Process. Process. A recent example of this in action is how the Boston marathon bomber was captured. Countless bits of data existed that each held a small piece of the clue, but independently were meaningless. Without collaboration among government and private agencies, the general public and law enforcement, and without appreciation for the nuance of what the data was saying, the investigation would have taken much longer. One of our clients, a manufacturing firm who builds control devices for automated production lines, hired us to train their executive team how to attend to process as well as content. Within one year they saved $50,000 on team meeting time alone. This number was calculated by multiplying the hourly rate of each executive by the reduced number of hours they spent wading through the usual data, reviewing the usual reports, making the usual decisions.

Content and Process cannot exist without each other. To act as if they do is self-deception and a recipe for disaster. To believe that content can speak for itself is delusion. To embrace the relationship and master it is the key to success, which brings us to the third reason to pay careful attention to process.

Process is a Competitive Advantage

Daniel Pink's book, *A Whole New Mind: Why Right-Brainers Will Rule the Future*, was published in 2005 and has been a long-running *New York Times* and *Business Week* bestseller that has been translated into 20 languages.[2] The significance of this book is its elegant articulation of a fundamental shift taking place regarding what it takes to be successful.

In the Agricultural Age, farmers ruled with their knowledge and experience of how to generate food. In the Industrial Age, factory workers ruled with their mastery of logic, efficiency, and linear mechanics. The Information Age was ruled by knowledge workers who could crunch data and find patterns. Pink argues that since the Industrial Age, left-brained competencies of linear, logical and rational thinking

---

2 Pink, D. (2005). *A Whole New Mind: Moving from the Information age to the Conceptual age.* Penguin Group, New York, NY

have been sufficient for the United States to maintain a competitive advantage in the world.

No longer, says Pink. Why? Because three prevailing trends are increasingly making left-brain competencies commonplace. First is the trend of Abundance. In our consumer-oriented society, people have too many choices – very little is scarce. Therefore, we're able to get everything we want at the lowest price. The second trend is Asia. Everything that can be outsourced and done more cheaply by someone else, is. The third trend is Automation, the proliferation of computerization, robots and technology.

According to Pink, these trends lead to three crucial questions for the success of any business:

1. Can a computer do it faster?
2. Is what I'm offering in demand in an age of abundance?
3. Can someone overseas do it more cheaply?

We are in a new era, argues Pink, called the Conceptual Age. In the Conceptual Age, creativity and empathy become competitive differences that can differentiate products and services. In other words, Content is the commodity; creativity and empathy are the Process by which that commodity is differentiated.

Pink suggests six new competencies that will increasingly be in demand in the Conceptual Age. All of these competencies are managed primarily from the right side of the brain. Below are brief descriptions of the six competencies with our own commentary in parentheses.

Design: Moving beyond function to engage the senses. Instead of just focusing on what the product can do (content), we must also pay attention to the full experience of using the product (process).

Story: No longer are people satisfied just by logical arguments (content); they want to be part of a story, a narrative that has meaning and purpose (process).

Symphony: Beyond just focusing on the details (content), people want to see inventions that create a beautiful blending of elements and bigger picture thinking (process).

Empathy: Beyond logical arguments (content), people want to be engaged emotionally and at an intuitive level (process).

Play: Beyond the organized and predictable (content), people want to experience a lighthearted humanness in their experience with products and services (process). Play, after all, is the rawest and most transparent of human experiences.

Meaning: Beyond an inanimate object (content), people want to be part of journey that has purpose, to participate in giving meaning to life beyond themselves (process).

Pink makes a compelling argument that companies who leverage these six new right-brain competencies will increasingly have a competitive edge in the conceptual age. And, there is significant overlap with the social-emotional intelligence competencies described earlier.

Welcome to the Process Age

While we agree with Pink's analysis, and we see mounting evidence to support his predictions, we believe that the next significant shift is already underway. Indeed, a balance between right-brained and left-brained competencies will be necessary to give companies a competitive edge in the global economy. And, there's more. Because the stakes are so high with current human global content capacity, process skills must reach beyond individual companies, product lines, marketing campaigns, and even national economic policy. And, they must reach down to the most intimate and personal relationships between parents and children, teachers and students, leaders and employees. This is one reason that this book can't focus on just leadership or just personal relationships. All of our behavior and relationships are connected and interdependent. @ HMMS, can't separate Pers & Prof

Even with these new brain competencies, we can only thrive within a larger context of accountable communities, socially responsible alliances, networks of mutually respectful organizations, and nations that trust each other. We no longer live in an age where national borders define our allegiances and alliances. Human connectedness and capacity has transcended all previous boundaries. That's the content. How we negotiate this emerging new world will require the mastery of process like never before. For this reason, we've named this era the Process Age. Briefly, here's the logic.

> The content of human knowledge and technology has the capacity to save us or destroy us;
> Process preceeds content;
> Relationships are paramount; and
> People and organizations who master process skills within relationships will have the ability to make the biggest difference in our world.

This book is our attempt to offer tools for the Process Age so that individuals, teams and organizations can begin developing their capacity and find inspiration through better process. So far, we have explained the crucial distinction between content and process. We have argued that process is a powerful force in human interaction. We've shared our reasons why process is more important than ever and why it's time for a book dedicated to process skills. From here we can begin to map a course for personal and professional discovery, growth, and inspiration.

Let's get specific about Drama.

CHAPTER 3

Understanding the Drama Triangle

In the classic Star Wars movies, *The Dark Side* was the metaphor for the part within in each of us that has the potential to bring harm to ourselves or others, especially those who are closest to us. Darth Vader was Princess Lea's father. The dark side is most certainly not your best self. It shows up when you travel down the wrong path, ending up with a distortion of your true character. Darth Vader ultimately acted within his true character by saving Luke Skywalker, and we will take a closer look at this emergence of one's "best self" later in the book. First, we will focus on the dark side of human behavior and interaction. After all, it's the suffering caused by this dark side of us that motivates us to do better.

Like Darth Vader, each of us shows the world our dark side behaviors, behaviors that are not in line with our best selves. We have all done things that brought harm to ourselves or someone in our lives. What does it look like when we show our dark side? As Darth Vader did, we cover up our best selves with a mask, a false role. Occasionally, when I (Jeff) am driving to work and get cut off by an inconsiderate motorist, I flip him the bird. I have just played a role, in this case, the role of an aggressive, entitled guy. The role into which I slipped temporarily is not my true, best self. Nonetheless, I am capable of going there in an instant, even without conscious awareness.

First we will illuminate dynamics of the dark side and then the positive alternatives that represent our best selves. This will set the stage for our journey of recognizing drama, choosing healthier alternatives, and inviting others to join us.

The Drama Triangle

In 1968, Dr. Steven Karpman discovered and named the Drama Triangle to describe unhealthy roles that people play when they are in distress. For this work, he was awarded in 1972 the Eric Berne Memorial Scientific Award by the International Transactional Analysis Association. Still today, the Drama Triangle remains one of the most elegant and practical models to understand dysfunctional interpersonal dynamics. It is the core, centering framework from which we begin nearly all our client work. We will use Karpman's Drama Triangle to begin our exploration of how things can go wrong in relationships, and then map a course and offer process-based tools to help get things back on track for you and the relationships in which you work and live.

The Drama Triangle is a model of how people relate to one another in distress, dysfunction, and conflict. We define distress as patterns of behavior we show when we are attempting to get some critical need met in unhealthy ways, usually through seeking negative attention. Drama is how humans negatively seek attention, meaning, and purpose when under the influence of distress. Drama most often involves predictable, habitual roles and accompanying behaviors. Our formal definition goes like this:

> *Drama is the pattern of habitual and predictable roles that cover up our best selves, justified by myths, which move us further away from solutions, healthy relationships, and effectiveness.*

In distress, we slip into roles virtually without awareness, behave in predictable ways that cover up our best selves, and believe myths about ourselves and others that it's OK to act this way. The result is a distorted sense of reality and responsibility to others for our behavior.

Eventually Darth Vader convinced himself he was doing the right and best thing. When I flipped off that driver I felt justified that it was what I needed to do and that the other driver deserved it.

It didn't help. I only became more upset and the other driver went on about his day. Did I feel justified? Yes. Did I cover up my best self? Definitely.

All of us have been in distress and have committed crimes of Drama. The good news is that this book will show you how to detect and navigate away from Drama in your life and negotiate the Darth Vaders in your world.

The Drama Triangle shown in Figure 1 is comprised of three roles: Persecutor, Rescuer, and Victim. By definition, a person in the Drama Triangle is in distress and occupies at least one of these roles, sometimes switching to another as the severity of distress increases.[1]

A Persecutor attacks verbally and/or blames; a Rescuer overdoes for someone else, reinforcing over-dependency; a Victim is over-adaptive or feels hurt when attacked or blamed. Let's take a look at each role in detail, exploring how they co-exist to perpetuate drama and dysfunction.

---

1 Karpman defines that drama is occurring once a person switches roles on the Drama Triangle. This is what causes unpredictability, second-guessing, and instability in relationships, and keeps the drama going. Transactional Analysis theory identifies the numerous games people play in the Drama Triangle, along with how people switch on each other.

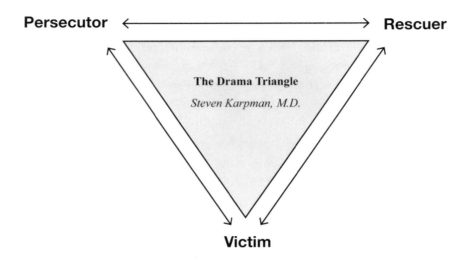

Figure 1: The Drama Triangle; Steven Karpman, M.D. (1968).

The Persecutor

Let's begin with the Persecutor. In this role we verbally attack or blame others, taking the position that "I'm OK, you are NOT OK." It may sound something like this:

> "Can't you do anything right?"
> "What is wrong with you!?"
> "You always screw up!"
> "What do we pay you for?"
> "Are you ever going to learn?"
> "You are so stupid."
> "You'll never amount to anything!"
> "It's your fault."
> "If it weren't for you..."
> "I didn't do it."
> "You made me do it."

When we adopt the Persecutor role, we lash out at others with our light saber, with the intention of harming them and righteously prevailing, thereby reinforcing our belief that we are OK and they are not. In the Persecutor role, we believe the illusion that the other person deserves what's coming to them and that we are justified in attacking or blaming. WOW! This role certainly has the potential to harm relationships.

I (Jeff) had a supervisor at one time in my life who was chronically in distress and frequently played the role of Persecutor. Whenever I brought him my written reports, he would get his red pen busy and tear them apart. No, I wasn't in grade school, I was in my thirties with a master's degree and a state license to practice social work. "This is not good enough," he would say dismissively. "Your writing is sub par." He offered no helpful feedback and made no comments about positive aspects of my work. I soon stopped taking my work to him and found other avenues for constructive feedback and self-improvement.

A parent in the Persecutor role might look at her child's report card, focus on the lowest grade, and critically attack with comments such as, "You really disappointed us by not getting better grades." All the while, she believes the illusion that focusing on what's wrong, criticizing, and inviting the child to feel guilty is the only way to improve performance, and that she is doing this because she know what's best.

A husband playing the Persecutor role might critically attack his wife, saying, "You could fit a lot more dishes in the dishwasher. What's wrong with you?"

The child in the Persecutor role may blame others by saying "It's not my fault I got kicked out of class. Johnny dared me to throw that spit wad." A friend in the Persecutor role might go on the attack by saying, "You should have called me and told me about the party last night. It's your fault I didn't make it."

An organization operating in the Persecutor role might institute policies that threaten employees to perform, believing that fear and guilt are the best motivators. A supervisor in such an organization might say things such as "You left me no choice but to fire you," or "If it weren't for your behavior, we wouldn't be in this mess."

Each position in the Drama Triangle needs fuel to function, much like the pistons in an engine. Drama is fueled by a distorted sense of reality and responsibility. When this illusion becomes habitual and is used to justify behavior, it is called a *Myth*. Taibi Kahler, a developmental psychologist, has made brilliant contributions to the understanding of Drama in relationships through his Process Communication Model® (PCM). Among his many contributions to the understanding of personality, communication, and distress dynamics, Kahler identified four myths that fuel drama and distress.[2] The fuel for the Persecutor is the myth "I believe I can make you feel bad emotionally." This myth justifies the belief that if I attack you, you will feel bad and do what I want. Or, if I blame you, you will feel bad and take over responsibility for me.

See if you can detect the myth "I believe I can make you feel bad emotionally" in the following statements:

"You really disappointed us by not getting better grades."
"You embarrassed me by hurting your mother's feelings that way in public."
"Tell him that. It will make him mad."
"Make her jealous."
"I'll never trust a man (woman) again and have them hurt me like that."

2 Taibi Kahler postulates that when we are in distress and playing a role in the Drama Triangle, we are believing one or more of Four Myths (Kahler 2008, Process Therapy Model), and he has identified the "offering" role and the "targeted" role in the other person to complete the symbiotic miscommunication.

Although beyond the scope of this book, Kahler's research also found significant correlations between personality type and the roles and behaviors on the Drama Triangle.[3]

Table 1 outlines characteristic behaviors and the myth accompanying the Persecutor role.

Persecutor Behaviors	Myth
Blaming, negatively complaining, sarcastic, manipulative, disregard for rules, critical, over-controlling, accusatory, suspicious, self-righteous, judgmental	"I can make you feel bad emotionally."

Table 1: Characteristics of the Persecutor Role

The Victim

In the Drama Triangle, Victims play the "poor me" card, overadapting, believing that things never turn out in their favor and that they don't deserve to get what they want most. They tolerate and often accept the behavior of the Persecutor. This is the person who frequently puts himself down, talks about how bad off she has it, or gives off the impression that he is worthless. The Victim is a Persecutor's dream come true!

People playing the Victim role rarely recognize that they choose to be helpless — that they choose not to advocate or initiate for themselves.

---

3 Taibi Kahler in his 2008 book, *Process Therapy Model*, explains his research correlating personality with specific, predictable distress behaviors, psychological issues and needs behind these behaviors, how they relate to the roles on the Drama Triangle, as well as specific interventions to invite a person out of distress and stop playing the role.

Common statements from a Victim include:

"It is too hard."
"I am never good enough."
"I always get it wrong."
"I am just no good."
"You are always right."
"If it wasn't for you, I'd be sunk."
"You always make me feel so good."

Victims play out this role as an invitation for others to rescue (save) or persecute (attack and blame) them. In the workplace we see this as the person who feels singled out for criticism, is always tired, always has home issues causing her trouble, and is rarely happy about her life. The bumper sticker, "Life's a bitch, then you die," rings true for people in the Victim role. It's easy to feel sorry for the Victim and want to either come to his rescue or criticize him for his plight. It might be counterintuitive, even heretical, to suggest that the Victim is responsible for his/her situation.

The Victim role is fueled by two myths; *"I believe you can make me feel bad emotionally,"* and *"I believe you can make me feel good emotionally."* Both myths imply that a third person or situation is in charge of their feelings, and lead Victims to give power over their "OK-ness" to others. They become emotional puppets, allowing other players in the Drama Triangle to pull their strings. Characteristic behaviors and myths associated with the Victim role are shown in Table 2.

Victim Behaviors	Myth
Suffering passively, complaining without doing anything, being self-critical, withdrawing, losing assertiveness, having weak boundaries, engaging in wishful thinking, being needy	"You can make me feel good emotionally." "You can make me feel bad emotionally."

Table 2: Characteristics of the Victim

The Rescuer

The third position on the Drama Triangle is the Rescuer. Persons playing this role are often seen as meddlers, inserting themselves in others' business. They especially gain a sense of satisfaction when they can intervene between Persecutors and Victims, hoping to save the day by fixing others' problems.

When you play a Rescuer role, you enable others to become dependent on you. You involve yourself with others in ways that don't encourage them to become competent, confident, and independent. You seem to get involved in everyone's problems except your own. This is the parent who takes the homework to school when the child leaves it at home; the employee who takes on additional work to cover for her coworker who is not pulling his weight; the friend who is forever giving advice even when it's not asked for.

While being rescued by others might feel good at first, it eventually leads to feelings of resentment. Strangely, Rescuers are often welcomed with open arms because of how convenient and easy it is to let them think and do for us. A parent can slip into this role easily with children and overfunction for them with comments such as, "I see you did not wear a coat, so I packed one for you." A co-worker can do the same with comments such as, "You didn't make it to the meeting so I looked up your report and handed it in for you." The Rescuer has a very difficult time tolerating the struggles of others who are experiencing natural consequences of their behavior. Rather than support and empower, they are tempted to give unsolicited advice or take over.

Common statements from a Rescuer include:

"Maybe you should try this."
"Don't you think this is a better option?"
"Shouldn't we stay in for dinner tonight?"
"Are you really going to wear that to school?"
"Why don't you try this..."
"I went ahead and proof-read that memo for you."

Unfortunately, rescuing prevents growth and learning. Experiencing the consequences of not having a coat on a cold day, being hungry because a meal was skipped, or figuring out one's own solution can be positive learning experiences. We believe that much of the entitled and egocentric behavior in younger generations comes from being rescued by their Baby Boomer parents.[4]

In the work environment Rescuers can easily become overworked, tired, and burned out because they cannot tolerate the discomfort of letting their peers experience negative consequences. It is common to hear a co-worker in the Rescuer role say, "If I don't pick up the slack, they will get into trouble," or a supervisor say, "I'll call her at home to remind her about the deadline."

The Rescuer has a very difficult time coping with his own and others' negative emotions when natural consequences occur. A parent of one of my (Jeff's) patients once told me that he did not want his son to experience failure. What? Failure and consequences are growth

---

4 For more on generational differences, we invite you to visit next-element.com, and search "generational differences."

opportunities that are often short-circuited by Rescuers. I (Jeff) worked at a residential home for boys who were in foster care and there was a rule made by a supervisor in the Rescuer role that the boys could not go outside in the winter without coats on. Here is what the boys figured out; refuse to wear a coat and I don't have to go to school. Here is what they did not learn; when my body is cold and there is a resource to help with this pain (a coat), I can then use the resources that are at my disposal and even ask for help. This story is not about the coat. It is about a rescuer who attempts to prevent pain for others and does not let them learn and grow. The boys were now focused on getting out of school rather than figuring out how to keep warm and attend school. Before long we had a facility full of boys who figured out how to get out of school. Just forget your coat!

I (Nate) had a supervisor who would frequently send advance notices to other members of our team if she thought I was going to bring up a potentially conflictual topic so as to "grease the skids" for me. I never asked her to do that. I was capable of dealing with transparent communication and potential conflict between all members of management team. The implicit invitation in her behavior was for me to feel grateful for her unsolicited "help" and play the role of Victim.

If you are a therapist, coach, facilitator or leader, what do you do when the person you are with begins to cry. Do you grab a tissue and give it to them? This is rescuing. When I (Nate) stopped handing my patients tissues and started allowing them to reach for the box, I saw noticeable changes in their self-confidence.

Supervisors trapped in the role of Rescuer cannot hold people accountable by leaving well enough alone. They choose to give an employee "one more chance" or save them from themselves. Often what happens instead is that the Rescuer will give chance after chance while picking up the slack themselves because they choose to avoid helping that person be accountable. The end result — ethical violations, broken policies, side conversations, cover-ups, and secrets.

One of the most difficult challenges for the Rescuer is being assertive. They choose *not* to say,

> *"I will support you, but I won't do it for you."*
> *"I am not going to bring your homework to school."*
> *"Will you go talk to him directly?"*
> *"You are fired for not meeting your responsibilities."*

What fuels the Rescuer's behavior? The myth behind their role is, "I believe I can make you feel good emotionally." The distorted rationale is that if I do or think for you, you will feel good, do what I want, and I can avoid negative feelings myself." The distorted reasoning fueled by this myth might sound like this:

> *"If I take your homework to school, then you will feel good and not get in trouble."*
> *"If I give you my coat then you will feel good and not be cold."*
> *"If I do your work, the boss will feel good and you won't get fired. Then you will feel good too."*
> *"If I give you advice, then I can make you successful and you will feel good."*
> *"If I don't fire you or hold you accountable, I can make you feel good and maybe you will perform better."*

Another manifestation of this myth is the attempt to protect someone from difficult feelings. Statements like, "It's going to be ok," "You are alright" or "It will be fine, it's not that big a deal," all suggest that I believe I can manage your feelings, therefore getting you to comply with my expectations, avoid the real issue, or avoid my own feelings. Ultimately, the Rescuer inhibits others from learning, growing, tolerating their own difficult emotions, and becoming responsible and independent. Their behaviors work against what it means to be emotionally intelligent.

Table 3 shows Rescurer behaviors and the accompanying myth.

Rescuer Behaviors	Myth
Giving unsolicited advice, covering for others, trying to "make it OK," doing others' job for them, meddling	"I can make you feel good emotionally."

Table 3: Characteristics of the Rescuer

The Persecutor, Victim, and Rescuer fit together in a dirty dance of drama, avoiding meaningful and honest conversation, creating unhealthy alliances, supporting secrecy, and diverting precious energy away from the most important things. In the next chapter we'll explore how this dance results in a self-fulfilling prophecy for everyone involved and how everyone loses in the process.

Aren't we all a little of all 3 (@ times?

CHAPTER 4

Drama: A Self-Fulfilling Prophecy

W e've suggested that Drama involves a distortion of responsibility and power. Let's dig a little deeper. In healthy relationships we are responsible to ourselves and others for our behavior. Responsibility to others means that we are accountable to our communities, families, and teams. Accountable for our behaviors means owning our choices, our attitudes, and our consequences.

Drama, Responsibility, and Power Plays

Let's explore how issues of responsibility become distorted in drama. In distress, the roles of the Drama Triangle cross the line, confuse the *to* and *for* part of responsibility, and are driven by the myths behind the roles. Along with the distortion of responsibility each role in the Drama Triangle attempts a power play by giving up its own power or attempting to hijack another person's power. The chart below describes the nature of irresponsibility and power plays associated with each myth.

Myth	Irresponsible Behavior	Power Play
"I believe I can make you feel bad emotionally."	Assuming too much responsibility for another's feelings and behaviors.	Trying to take power away from another person through efforts to control.

Myth	Irresponsible Behavior	Power Play
"I believe I can make you feel good emotionally."	Assuming too much responsibility for another's feelings and behaviors.	Trying to take power away from another person through efforts to fix.
"I believe you can make me feel bad emotionally."	Assuming too little responsibility for your own feelings and behaviors.	Giving up your own power by allowing others' efforts to control you.
"I believe you can make me feel good emotionally."	Assuming too little responsibility for your own feelings and behaviors.	Giving up your own power by allowing others' efforts to fix you.

Table 1: Myths, Irresponsible Behavior, and Power Plays

All power plays in the Drama Triangle are illusions based on the myths. The irony of drama is that regardless of your role, when you believe and act on one of the four myths, you actually lose power because you are under the influence of the myth. In drama you give up and give over your power to the myth. You rely on your role to get what you want even though you are harming yourself and others. When you act outside the realm of your best character, you lose power over yourself. The distorted power you believe you have comes from believing in the myths. It's all an illusion in the long run.

The irony cuts still deeper. In drama, people are seduced by the false sense of control that comes from believing the myths. A Victim feels powerful when she is needy and people come to her rescue. A Persecutor feels powerful when he frightens subordinates into complying with a policy. A Rescuer feels powerful when somebody comes running to her for help and she saves the day. Unfortunately, these power plays are doomed because they originate from myths. As we all know, the long-term consequences of relating to others in drama are catastrophic to personal relationships, organizational morale and productivity, and global alliances.

Drama is a Self-Fulfilling Prophecy

Why is the Drama Triangle so seductive? Because it is self-fulfilling, self-justifying, and self-perpetuating. The myths and associated behaviors of the roles become a self-fulfilling prophecy and are self-justifying. Every role seeks to have things turn out in its favor — that is, in a way that supports its particular myth. Later we will explore the phenomenon of self-justification in depth.

No one wants to be alone in the Drama Triangle. The Drama Triangle has a very active and well-funded recruiting department! Misery loves company, and much like the Bermuda Triangle, drama sucks others in and creates a vortex from which it's very difficult to escape. As we explore the dimensions of drama in more depth in this chapter, we will show how drama invites more drama.

Finally, drama is a self-perpetuating cycle because each role complements the other roles, feeding off each other and perpetuating the self-fulfilling nature of the myths. Let's take a look at how each myth subtly recruits for positions in the drama dance.[1]

Myth	Roles Being Recruited
I believe I can make you feel bad emotionally.	Persecutor recruiting a Victim
I believe I can make you feel good emotionally.	Rescuer recruiting a Victim
I believe you make me feel bad emotionally.	Victim recruiting a Persecutor
I believe you can make me feel good emotionally.	Victim recruiting a Rescuer

Table 2: Myths and Roles being recruited in Drama

---

1 Taibi Kahler describes these dynamics in detail in his book, *Process Therapy Model.*

When roles match up, they can get along famously and justify one another's behaviors and existence. Here are some examples:

> **Supervisor (P):** "You better get this done before you leave today, or else!"
>
> **Employee (V):** "Ok, I will stay late," (even though last week the employee asked to leave early today to see her son play soccer today).

Both persons support the illusion, play their role, and perpetuate their Myths.

> **Peer 1 (R):** "I will go ahead and get that paper work completed for you. I know that you are tired and worn out today."
>
> **Peer 2 (V):** "Thanks. I never seem to be able to get my paperwork done on time."

In this example the Victim plays along, allowing the Rescuer to rescue him from the consequences of his own choices.

> **Supervisor** (R): "It seems you're late a lot. Here is a list of tips I found on time management."
>
> **Employee** (V): "I just can't make this schedule work because I can never get out of bed and I am always so tired in the mornings."
>
> **Supervisor** (R): "OK. I'll call you in the morning before I leave for work."
>
> **Employee** (V): "I guess. I don't know what I'd do without you."

In this example, the supervisor fails to assertively confront the performance problems, instead rescuing the employee from taking responsibility for his actions. The employee plays the complimentary Victim role.

Son (V) calls dad: "I ran out of gas and I'm stranded. I don't know what to do."

Dad (P): "I'm not coming to get you. It's about time you grow up and learn how to take care of yourself. Think before you act next time!"

Son (V) calls Mom: "I am so dumb and I ran out of gas and Dad is angry."

Mom (R): "I'll be right there."

Later, when everyone is at home...

Dad (P): "What's wrong with you, son? Didn't you think to look at the gas gauge?"

Son (V): "You are right, Dad. I am such a dummy."

Mom (R): "Honey, I will put money in the glove box so that you will always have money for gas if you forget to look at the gas gauge again."

Dad (P): "Don't coddle the boy! He needs to grow up and learn the hard way".

Mom (R) (to son): "It's OK, honey."

Son escapes to his room to listen to the rest of the argument that supports his myth, "You can make me feel bad emotionally." In this scenario, nobody gets the opportunity to be responsible, and the likelihood of anyone changing his or her behavior is nonexistent. As these dynamics repeat themselves many times a day for years, all participants become more and more convinced that their role IS their identity. No wonder family systems are so hard to change, and why they perpetuate through generations. Drama is a self-perpetuating cycle that is very difficult to break.

Enabling and Drama

Enabling simply means that you contribute to keeping the problem alive, maintaining dysfunction, avoiding responsibility. Which role on the Drama Triangle do you believe is the biggest enabler? Many people mistakenly assume the Rescuer is the biggest enabler because it's easy to see how they prevent people from taking personal responsibility for their behavior. But in fact, every role enables the others. Every role needs the others to function, and none of them invite appropriate responsibility for self to others.

Four Choices in Drama

It seems that most of life is lived in the Drama Triangle. Are we doomed? Not at all. We always have choices. The secret is in recognizing and owning the choices you make. Here are a few options.

Option 1: Run Away!

You can try to avoid it, escape, pretend it's not there, or act like you're unaffected. This is very difficult because drama is tenacious, insidious, and powerful. Each role in the Drama Triangle is looking for its justification, the payoff for getting other roles to play along. And remember, like the Mob, drama will find you. It will be waiting for you where you least expect it.

Option 2: Assume the Position

You can play along and fill a complimentary role, doing what you've always done, playing the role like you've rehearsed so many times before, and doing your part to keep the drama alive. Hey, it may be painful, but it's predictable! You know what to do, and you know how it turns out. It's human nature.

Option 3: I'll See Your Drama and Raise It One!

You could try to compete for a role, playing King of the Hill with your colleagues, family, or boss. Or you could try to beat them to the punch, seeing who can dominate a particular drama role first. We see this all too often in the family, workplace, or community. It is at times tragic and other times comical. When Victim roles compete, it's a contest for who can be the biggest loser. When Persecutors compete, people get hurt. When Rescuers compete, it's like immature adolescent boys trying to get noticed by the new girl in town.

Option 4: A Compassionate Alternative

Choose not to play the game while also grappling with the real issues. There are options that invite others out of drama while keeping you on safe soil. If you're interested in this option, read on.

The Solution

CHAPTER 5

A Compassionate Alternative to Drama

L et's return to the Stars Wars theme. What is the alternative to the Dark Side? The Force, of course! Luke Skywalker chooses to use the positive power of his true, best self, The Force, unlike Darth Vader, who chooses to act from the dark side of his nature. We all have both of these potentials within us. We can choose which one to call on.

The Compassion Triangle

The alternative to the Drama Triangle, suggests Steven Karpman, is the Compassion Triangle. The Compassion Triangle suggests a framework for moving into open dialogue, problem solving, and conflict resolution. In this mode, you are able to utilize your best self — your personal "Force."

Compassion should not be misconstrued as a touchy-feely, anything goes, hug-a-thug approach. The Latin root of the word *compassion* means "to struggle with." Compassion is difficult. It requires perseverance, humility, and skill.

In the Compassion Triangle, the positions of Persecutor, Rescuer, and Victim are complemented by the skill sets of Persistence, Resourcefulness, and Vulnerability, respectively. We've chosen to rename Vulnerability as Openness due to the negative connotations associated with vulnerability in Western culture. Figure 1 shows Karpman's Compassion Triangle.

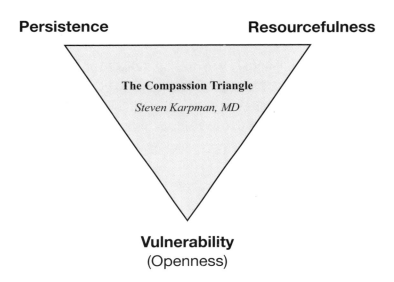

Persistence   **Resourcefulness**

The Compassion Triangle

Steven Karpman, MD

Vulnerability
(Openness)

Figure 1. The Compassion Triangle; Steven Karpman, MD (1968)

Openness

Openness is the alternative to being a Victim and is characterized by confident transparency, honesty, assertiveness, and the willingness to risk trusting another person. Being open means knowing that my OK-ness is not dependent upon another's response, rejecting the myth that "You can make me feel good or bad, emotionally."

Persistence

Persistence describes perseverance and courage — the willingness to stick with someone or something rather than attack, abandon, or blame. Being persistent means holding self and others accountable in a way that preserves the dignity and respect of all parties, rejecting the myth that "I can make you feel bad emotionally."

Resourcefulness

Resourcefulness involves creative problem solving, flexibility, and adaptability in the face of obstacles. Being resourceful in relationships means using problem-solving skills to help others empower themselves, rejecting the myth that "I can make you feel good emotionally by doing the thinking or doing for you." There's a saying, "If you give a man a fish, he'll eat for a day. If you teach him how to fish, he'll eat for the rest of his life." This is the difference between Rescuing (give a man a fish) and Resourceful (teach him how to fish).

Roles vs. Skill Sets

Let's clarify the difference between the roles/positions in the Drama Triangle and the skill-sets in the Compassion Triangle. Roles are habitual, heavily influenced by past experiences, and predictable. Skill sets can be learned, practiced, and applied to increase effectiveness. While we may play one or two typical roles when we are in distress, we are capable of developing all three compassion skill sets for effective functioning. Table 1 provides a more detailed distinction between positions/roles and skill sets.

Positions/Roles	Skill-Sets
Prescribed	Dynamic and Adaptive
Habitual	Responsive
Involve Duty and Expectations	Involve Appropriate Application
Hard to Break	Can be Learned
Predictable	Applicable

Table 1: Distinction between Positions/Roles and Skill Sets

This is good news! You can develop each compassion skill-set to improve your effectiveness in dealing with whatever life throws at you.

How does compassion neutralize the negative pull of Drama? Like Yoda, people accessing the skills of Openness, Resourcefulness, and Persistence simultaneously keep themselves out of drama while offering a healthier alternative path for others. Primarily, they have let go of the myths, which is one of the most liberating and empowering things a human being can do.

"Letting go of myths is one of the most liberating and empowering things a human being can do."

What do you do when you see Drama approaching? The answer: Stay in the Compassion Triangle! Keep your power. Don't buy into the myths. Don't cover up the authentic you with power plays. Be responsible for you.

Let's look at some examples in which a person avoids being seduced into a drama role and instead utilizes the complementary compassion skill.

> **Drama invitation** (Persecutor): *What is wrong with you?*
> **Compassion response** (Persistent): *This is what works for me. Will you please not talk to me like that?*

> **Drama invitation** (Persecutor): *It's your fault I didn't get my paperwork done.*
> **Compassion response** (Persistent): *I got my work done. You are responsible for your work.*

Some of you may be saying, "This is too simple and it will never work!" Our response: Simple doesn't mean it's easy! However, with practice, we think you'll find it to be a very effective process. Drama is seductive, habitual, and reinforced throughout our lives. Choosing a compassionate alternative takes work, practice, and a willingness to let go of myths. Perhaps the hardest part of moving out of drama is letting go of the myths and the behavior that has supported them for so long.

Let's look at some other ways that compassion might respond to drama:

> **Drama invitation** (Rescuer): *"I went ahead and proof-read the memo for you."*
> **Compassion response** (Resourceful): *"I appreciate your willingness to help. Next time, I will ask you if I want help."*

Drama invitation (Rescuer): *"Don't you think you should fix more vegetables for dinner??*

Compassion response (Resourceful): *"What is your opinion about a balanced dinner for our family?"*

You may be asking yourself, "Shouldn't I acknowledge the complaint about working late or how hard she worked on dinner?" No. Don't get sucked into the content of dinner and work. It is not about that. The real issue is the process of your relationship. It's not what you talk about, but rather how you go about it that makes all the difference. In the Compassion Triangle we give primary attention to the relationship or the process of "us." When I thank you for dinner I am saying, "Thank you for your best self." I am honoring my responsibility *to* you. When I apologize for being late I am taking responsibility *for* my behavior. What if I had taken the bait and played the role? The Rescuer is looking for a Victim.

Drama invitation (Rescuer): *"I went ahead and proof-read the memo for you."*

Drama response (Victim): *"I am such a horrible speller, you should just do it next time."*

Drama invitation (Rescuer): *"I will proof-read all your memos from now on."*

Drama response (Victim): *"I don't know what I'd do without you to keep me from looking like a fool."*

In this exchange, notice how responsibility is short-circuited and both parties continue to believe in their myth. We could extend this example to many parent-child relationships. As a therapist I (Jeff) have worked with many a parent who rescued their child time and time again only to find their child unable to function independently as an adult.

Research on self-esteem[1] has shown that most self-esteem enhancing interventions of the 1980s and 1990s were a breeding ground for the Rescuer - Victim relationship. Consequently we are experiencing a generation of children who struggle to incorporate constructive criticism or learn from failure.

Let's look at ways to respond compassionately to the Victim.

Drama invitation (Victim): *"I will never be able to complete this project. I am in way over my head."*
Compassion response (Open): *"It is a tough project. I can imagine how overwhelmed you might be feeling."*

Drama invitation (Victim): *"I'll never be able to pass this test. I am so stupid."*
Compassion response (Open): *"You are capable and it will take hard work. I believe in you."*

A healthy exchange within the Compassion Triangle might look like this:

I am struggling with this project (Open). *Will you please help me with pages 4 thru 11?* (Resourceful)

Yes, I will help you and let's see if we can find some strategies that will help you later on, too. (Resourceful and Persistent)

So when you see a drama role approaching, the basic principle is to respond with the complementary compassionate response. Much like a martial artist deftly diverts negative energy and redirects it to his

1 Bushman, B.J. & Baumeister, R.F. (1998). "Threatened Egotism, Narcissism, Self-Esteem, and Direct and Displaced Aggression: Does Self-Love or Self-Hate Lead to Violence?" *Journal of Personality and Social Psychology;* Vol 75(1): 219-229.

benefit, the compassionate communicator meets each drama role with the complementary compassionate skill set. As Martin Luther King said: "A man can't ride your back unless it's bent."

Meet Victim with Openness. Meet Persecutor with Persistence. Meet Rescuer with Resourcefulness. Personal growth includes becoming aware of your own drama tendencies and developing skills and habits for choosing openness, resourcefulness, and persistence. The next two chapters offer specific guidelines for self-assessment of drama, and the rest of the book offers tools and perspectives for skill building.

By staying in the Compassion Triangle, you'll be able to respond to your community in healthy and constructive ways and not get sucked into drama. There is drama all around us, and we can make the choice of whether to accept the invitation into drama or offer compassionate invitations out of drama.

Chapter 8 will explore how we invite and influence. Positive change happens only through invitation and influence. We cannot force anybody to change. You know someone is in the drama triangle when you hear comments like "he made me do it," "that makes me angry," "she made me feel bad," or "I had no choice but to fire him." Each of these statements involve a myth and the illusion that someone or something has control over another person's feelings or behaviors. Desperate statements like this usually reveal a compassion skill deficit.

The Drama Triangle has been extremely powerful for adding clarity and directing focus in our work doing organizational development, training, and professional consulting across multiple contexts, industries, and age groups. In reviewing our experience with counseling, coaching, consulting, facilitating culture change, and leadership development, we have seen that our clients consistently desire these outcomes:

trust
team cohesion
transparency

self-awareness
perseverance
tenacity
courage
innovation
creative problem solving
optimism

This list is all about Openness, Resourcefulness, and Persistence.

Current research on resilience, hope, leadership skills, social-emotional intelligence, positive psychology, and stress coping consistently point to the importance of healthy openness, resourcefulness, and persistence as characteristics of adaptive and successful functioning. Whether your area of interest is personal growth, student achievement, team building, or leadership development, these dimensions are relevant and necessary.

Moving from drama to compassion can happen when you avoid getting sucked into drama and chose to respond by staying in the Compassion Triangle. This choice revolves around being responsible *to* others *for* your own behaviors.

CHAPTER 6

Dimensions of Drama: The Big Three

Consider a continuum called "approach to life," in which the depths of drama rule at one end and the heights of compassion triumph at the other. Between these two extremes are many hills and valleys. The journey from drama to compassion and back is a process that happens many times a day with individuals, teams, and even entire organizations and governments. Thus far, we have outlined the characteristic roles and dynamics of drama and the signature skill sets of compassion, and offered examples of how these responses to life show up in our lives.

In the next two chapters we will explore the continuum between drama and compassion from a variety of angles, offering a series of perspectives to help readers understand what's really going on in human interaction and what predictable behaviors and attitudes to expect. At the end of each section we offer a simple checklist to determine where you are along the continuum. This chapter outlines the three primary ways in which our thoughts, feelings, and actions deteriorate in drama — namely, through tunnel vision, self-justification, and the cultivation of delusion. In the next chapter, we dive deeper into six additional dimensions of drama that we've discovered in our work with organizations and individuals seeking to make lasting change in behaviors, relationships, and work culture. Taken together, these two chapters will help you, your team, or your organization assess where drama and compassion are present. Moving forward, we will offer practical and specific strategies for moving from drama to compassion in your personal and professional life.

Let's begin by looking at how drama and compassion affect our viewpoint on life.

Perspective vs. Tunnel Vision

"A little perspective, like a little humor, goes a long way"

– Allen Klein

As a ten-year-old boy growing up in rural Kansas, I (Nate) remember the first time my friends and I climbed the local grain elevator in our town. Defying the clearly posted signs to keep off, we scampered our way up the enclosed ladder to the top of the one hundred foot high silo. When we came out on top, besides being petrified by the height, I recall being astounded by the view. I saw things I'd never seen before in my own town. I understood relationships between buildings that were now obvious from this vantage point. I saw into backyards of neighbors I had always wondered about. This new perspective changed my life. Since then I've always been curious about what I might be missing, what else is out there, what I can't see from where I stand.

A friend of mine Steve flies helicopters. While he was in training for his license, he was required to log a certain number of hours of flight time each month. Once he was cleared to fly solo, he invited friends to join him on his Saturday morning jaunts from Wichita, Kansas to Ponca City, Oklahoma where small aircraft pilots from around the region congregated every week for a breakfast buffet at the city airport. When it was my turn, I was excited for the chance to fly in a helicopter. My enthusiasm subsided somewhat when I discovered that the combined weight of Steve and me exceeded the operating limits of the ultralight helicopter by two pounds. I gave up my spot that week and vowed to lose enough weight that I could fly with him next time.

I did get my chance a month later, and came in just under the weight limit. We took off and made the 30-minute flight from Wichita to Ponca City. As we approached the airport, I could see planes of all sizes, shapes, and colors approaching and landing at the airport, much like a scene out of a sci-fi movie where flying vehicles crisscross an urban landscape of skyscrapers. We were the only helicopter in sight.

Steve approached what he claimed was the landing pad. It looked more like a patch of grass to me. He maneuvered the helicopter to one side, then the other. He eased the craft 180 degrees around and began coming down. Then, he climbed back up and took a different position. Becoming somewhat impatient for the breakfast buffet, I asked Steve what the holdup was. He explained that he was trying to adjust his attitude to ensure a safe landing.

This was not the answer I was expecting or wanted. Attitude? What's wrong with your attitude? I thought. And, for that matter, was something wrong with my attitude? "I have a good attitude", I assured him, not wanting to be responsible for a possible helicopter crash in front of all his buddies. And, that might mean I'd miss breakfast.

Steve explained what he meant. In aviation, attitude refers to how one approaches a landing. Helicopters have the ability to take off and land vertically, and many factors influence a landing, including wind speed and direction. And, what I didn't recognize was that the landing pad was in the middle of a recently-mowed field and was covered with dry hay. Steve explained that if his attitude was wrong, he could very well kick up a ton of hay that would blow right over onto the buffet line set up in the open hangar 50 yards away.

It all made sense then. The right attitude helps ensure the safety and respect of others when landing. For Steve, attitude was all about achieving a healthy perspective. For me, it was about having hay-free biscuits and gravy!

Perspective is the ability to see things from different vantage points, to view a problem from several angles and appreciate the impact of different approaches. Perspective is about seeing the forest and the trees, about appreciating the big picture as well as each element of that picture. Perspective is about keeping an open mind to possibilities, seeking out alternative views and holding them in awareness. Plato said that the height of wisdom is the ability to simultaneously entertain two opposing points of view. Whether it's looking at a neighborhood from 100 feet above ground or finding a safe approach to land an aircraft, perspective allows one to see more clearly and choose the best available option.[1]

The three qualities of compassion allow and facilitate perspective. Openness allows one to take in and accept new information and insights from others in order to more clearly see them for who they are. Resourcefulness allows for creative problem solving that embraces the possibility that there could be more than one way to solve a problem. Persistence gives new as well as old ideas a chance; it means refusing to discount or write off another person or idea just because it seems difficult or doesn't make sense at first.

---

1 This concept inspired the name of our company, Next Element. *Next* is not the same as new, or better, as that would imply throwing the baby out with the bath water. Next is about moving forward, keeping on with the journey. *Element* describes both the smallest component (e.g. elements in an atomic reaction) and an entire context that conspires to support optimum functioning, i.e. "I am in my element." Next Element is about transcending, including, and tending even to the small things that contribute to our larger life situation.

"Nothing is more dangerous than an idea, when it's the only one you have."

– Emile-Auguste Chartier

The drama contrast to perspective is tunnel vision. It is an inability to see more than one possibility at a time. If you've ever beat your head against a wall, trying the same thing over and over without success, you've experienced the frustration of tunnel vision.

Nonetheless, tunnel vision is a seductive state of being. It feels as though you have everything figured out and can see the solution. Unfortunately, being in the tunnel yourself prevents you from knowing what you don't know. Another disadvantage of tunnel vision is the loss of peripheral vision. This is true both literally and metaphorically. Research shows that optimists have better peripheral vision than pessimists. They can literally see more of life. No wonder optimists are routinely more successful, find more solutions, and enjoy life more fully. I (Nate) have been blessed with opportunities that only became visible when I approached things from a different perspective.

Overall, tunnel vision results in poor judgment, reduced problem solving ability, a mind closed to other perspectives and possibilities, and ultimately, impaired relationships and productivity.

Table 1 shows several pairs of statements describing behavior on either end of the drama-compassion continuum. To see where you are, complete this assessment. Better yet, ask a trusted friend or colleague fill it out it as they experience you. Make clear that you want their honest feedback. Remember, if you are experiencing tunnel vision, your perspective is impaired and others may have a more accurate picture of your behavior than you do.

For best results, use the following scoring method: for each pair of statements, you have 100 percentage points to split up between the two statements based on what percentage of the time you experience

63

each behavior. You must divide the entire 100 points between the two statements. (For example, for the first pair of statements, your colleague may estimate that you spend 60 percent of your time trying different approaches, and 40 percent trying the same thing over and over.) After you've rated all the statements, average your scores in each column for an overall ratio of how much time you spend in Drama vs. Compassion.[2]

Perspective (Compassion)	Tunnel Vision (Drama)
__ Tries different approaches, learning from mistakes along the way	__ Tries the same thing over and over even if it doesn't work
__ Encourages input from others	__ Discounts others' ideas or suggestions before giving them a try
__ Seems open-minded	__ Seems close-minded
__ Asks for help	__ Doesn't ask for help
_____ Perspective % Average	_____ Tunnel-Vision % Average

Table 1: Checklist for Perspective vs. Tunnel Vision

---

2 Or, complete Next Element's online Drama Assessment by going to drama.next-element.com. Get your scores, feedback, and helpful tips for making positive changes.

Effective vs. Justified

"Let go of your attachment to being right; and suddenly your mind is more open. You're able to benefit from the unique viewpoints of others, without being crippled by your own judgment."

—Ralph Marston

In the compassion triangle, being effective is prized, possible, and promoted. Effectiveness means keeping your eye on the prize, staying focused on goals, and getting the job done. In Patrick Lencioni's book, *The Five Dysfunctions of a Team*, he describes a hierarchy of team development competencies. At the top of the hierarchy, the highest evolution in a team, is what he calls "focus on results." When we focus on results, we put personal agendas aside, attend primarily to the good of the whole, and do not allow Drama to distract from bottom-line results. Effectiveness happens when we let go of ulterior motives that lurk in the Drama Triangle and become open to a greater purpose and possibility.

By contrast, seeking justification is the Drama-based opposite of acting effectively and represents an effort to maintain the illusion of control. The need to feel justified, to believe that "I was right," is one of the strongest human urges. Humans will go to great lengths to feel right, be right, and believe they are right, regardless of their role in drama.

Self-justification is the norm in the Drama Triangle. By playing the Victim role, you can feel justified in your belief that "nobody cares about me and I am worthless." By playing the Persecutor role, you can go to bed at night fully convinced that others are stupid, lazy, or uncommitted and are the cause of our troubles in this world. As a

Rescuer, you can easily convince yourself of the martyr's logic that others need you to save the day. When things turn out as you expect, you feel in control.

Unfortunately, in Drama the need to feel justified trumps effectiveness. So we routinely see persons making decisions and choosing behaviors to support their own Drama-based myths about themselves and others while being completely ineffective in the process. One signature sign of self-justification is the word *see*. "See, I told you so." "See, if you'd just have listened to me in the beginning." "See, I knew I couldn't do it." When used in this way, the word says nothing more than "I am right and you are wrong."

The need for self-justification is one of the primary forces behind the self-fulfilling prophecy and operates as a powerful invitation for others to join the drama party. Humans will go to great lengths, consciously and unconsciously, to influence the outcome of events so that their beliefs and expectations are validated, even about negative outcomes. Whether you worry yourself sick, overtly sabotage your teammates, or subscribe only to blogs that support your political views, the end result is that you can say, "See, I knew this would happen," and feel temporarily powerful. To learn more about the social science behind the self-fulfilling prophecy, we recommend the work of Albert Bandura on self-efficacy.[3] For a terrific summary of the research on how the self-fulfilling prophecy works in health and wellness, readers are referred to Robert Sapolsky's book, *Why Zebra's Don't Get Ulcers.*[4]

To find out where you are on the effective-justified continuum, ask a friend or colleague to rate you on the following checklist. Use the same scoring system as before.

3 Bandura, A. (1997). *Self-efficacy: The Exercise of Control.* New York: W.H. Freeman and Company.
4 Sapolsky, R. (1998) 3rd Ed. *Why Zebras Don't Get Ulcers.* Henry Holt & Co., New York, NY.

Effective (Compassion)	Justified (Drama)
__ Puts team goals above personal agendas	__ Pursues personal agendas at the expense of team goals
__ Admits mistakes	__ Uses words like "See", or "What you need to understand" to prove points
__ Can engage in passionate dialogue about ideas without attacking others	__ Attacks others who disagree or gives in quickly without taking a stand
__ Seeks out honest feedback	__ Avoids feedback or opposing views
____ Effective % Average	____ Justified % Average

Table 2: Checklist for Effective vs. Justified

In Touch with Reality vs. Delusional

"The definition of insanity is doing the same thing over and over again expecting different results."

—Albert Einstein

Perspective and Effectiveness create fertile conditions for getting, and staying, in touch with reality. Let's start by defining our terms. Being in touch with reality means that you can understand and appreciate that there might be different perspectives and approaches to a problem and that choosing to be effective might mean trying different approaches depending on the person or situation. In touch with reality involves a deep understanding of the human qualities in a situation; personalities, preferences, motivators, attitudes, values, and belief systems. It means being simultaneously aware of contextual factors such as rules, expectations, budget, time frames, and available resources. At the core, being in touch with reality begins by recognizing that your perception and perspective is only part of reality. It's about recognizing that *my truth* isn't the same as *the truth*.

Being in touch with reality requires considerable patience and tolerance for ambiguity. The qualities of Openness, Resourcefulness, and Persistence come in quite handy when the situation requires you to understand and reconcile multiple realities or truths.

As persons get caught up in the drama roles of Victim, Persecutor, or Rescuer, being in touch with reality slowly gives way to delusional belief systems. A natural consequence of tunnel vision and self-justification is that a person can begin to believe that they have it figured out and are right about their conclusions, even in the face of overwhelming evidence to the contrary. A delusion, by definition, is a well-developed and coherent belief system that drives one's behavior, is not shared by others, and not supported by the facts. It's the polar opposite of being in touch with reality. Movies often show characters with tunnel-vision.

One sign that a person is losing touch with reality is when he or she attempts to reduce things to binary categories, such as black or white, right or wrong, my way or the highway, us against them. The belief behind these statements indicates that the person cannot tolerate or negotiate the uncomfortably gray nature of reality and are coping by oversimplifying. Stereotyping and prejudice arise from such oversimplification.

The Drama Triangle supports delusional belief systems by reducing behavior to very predictable, simple, and limited categories — the roles of Persecutor, Rescuer, and Victim. Delusions can occur in any of the three roles. People playing the role of a Persecutor can develop paranoid beliefs that "if you're not with me, you're against me" and go on preemptive strikes within families, organizations, or entire countries. Those playing the Rescuer role can falsely believe that without them things would fall apart, and continue to try fixing things even when the evidence suggests nobody wants or appreciates their help, or that their behaviors are fostering passive dependency in others. When playing the role of Victim, peole can retreat into a place where they believe they are unconditionally unworthy and become suicidal.

Where do you stand on the in touch with reality-delusional continuum? Ask a friend or trusted colleague to rate you on the items below. Use the rating scale outlined earlier.

In Touch with Reality (Compassion)	Delusional (Drama)
__ Can articulate several approaches or perspectives	__ Argues or keeps advocating for only one approach
__ Has empathy for others' point of view	__ Unable to see things from another's point of view
__ Makes corrections when faced with new or contradicting evidence	__ Is unaffected by new or contradicting evidence
__ Remains open and calm when challenged	__ Becomes defensive when challenged
___ In Touch with Reality % Average	___ Delusional % Average

Table 3: Checklist for In Touch with Reality vs. Delusional

In the next chapter we'll explore six more dimensions of drama. These will give you a host of new perspectives and insights on how drama undermines our ability to be productive and maintain healthy relationships, as well as the effective alternatives of compassion. These two chapters offer you, your team, or your organization powerful tools to assess where you are now and what specific behaviors and attitudes you can nurture to lift you beyond drama.

For Next Element's online Drama Assessment, go to drama. next-element.com. Rate yourself, a peer or boss, your team, or your entire organization. Receive a personal report with implications and recommendations. Print out or e-mail your report, share it with others, or use it to guide your team discussions.

CHAPTER 7

Dimensions of Drama: The Rest of the Story

Six more dimensions complete our list of the ways Drama can suck the life and energy out of your relationships and organizations. As with the first three dimensions, we offer the compassionate alternative for each.

Forward Failing vs. Backward Failing

"Success consists of going from failure to failure without loss of enthusiasm."

—Winston Churchill

In his book, *Failing Forward: Turning Mistakes into Stepping Stones for Success*, John Maxwell[1] argues that the difference between average people and successful people is their perception of and response to failure. In the Compassion Triangle, failure truly becomes a stepping stone to success. Rather than paralyzing, it energizes. Rather than

---

1 Maxwell, J. (2000). *Failing Forward: Turning mistakes into stepping stones for success*. Thomas Nelson, Nashville, TN

creating fear, it creates opportunity. Maxwell's comparison of Forward Failing vs. Backward Failing is shown in Table 1. We invite you to use it as a personal checklist to see whether you are approaching failure from a drama or compassion perspective.

"Forward failing is a major driver of innovation."

Using the same rating scale from the previous chapter, split 100 percent into each pair of the statements and average your scores for an overall Forward Failing vs. Backward Failing score. Use this individually, as a 360-degree feedback process[2] or as a team-assessment tool.

Forward Failing (Compassion)	Backward Failing (Drama)
__ Taking responsibility	__ Blaming others
__ Learning from mistakes	__ Repeating mistakes
__ Knowing failure is a part of progress	__ Expecting to never fail again
__ Maintaining a positive attitude	__ Expecting to continually fail
__ Challenging outdated assumptions	__ Accepting tradition blindly
__ Taking new risks	__ Being limited by past mistakes
__ Believing something didn't work	__ Thinking, "I am a failure"
__ Persevering	__ Quitting
__ Forward Failing % Average	__ Backward Failing % Average

Table 1: Checklist for Failing Forward vs. Failing Backward

---

2 The number 360 represents ratings from multiple vantage points: e.g. from a peer, supervisor, and subordinate, to provide various perspectives.

Earlier we discussed an organization with whom we are working on a Patient Centered Medical Home initiative. One of the most effective practices they have implemented is called Rapid Cycle Change, a process of experimenting with small changes, evaluating effectiveness, and moving forward with adjustments quickly, maximizing practical learning. Medical teams are learning how to experiment, fail, learn, grow, and share their experience with others. Weekly, sometimes daily, medical teams share about what they've learned. Many processes are able to undergo four or five experimental revisions in several weeks, resulting in extremely high levels of practical utility and buy-in. Rapid Cycle Change only works where failure is considered normative rather than the exception. Forward failing is a major driver of innovation.

Leveraging Diversity vs. Abusing Diversity

"Stupidity is the attempt to iron out all differences and not to use or value them creatively."

—Bill Mollison

We are tired of hearing the phrase "tolerant of diversity." To us, it implies "I'll allow you to coexist with me, but I don't have to like it." In today's multicultural and multitalented workplace, merely tolerating differences is inadequate and inefficient. The most successful parents, teachers, leaders and organizations are those who are able to welcome and leverage diversity, truly transforming differences into assets. Accomplishing this requires a five-part skill set.

1. Curiosity and understanding of individual differences, including race, gender, ethnicity, sexual orientation, personality, motivational needs, communication and leadership preferences, and many other dimensions.

2. Awareness of how individual talents and characteristics impact others.

3. Genuine desire to see these differences utilized to benefit group or community goals.

4. Ability to connect with and motivate the people or groups who possess these unique gifts.

5. Ability to design projects, tasks, and environments that utilize a diverse range of gifts.

Companies like Google, Patagonia, Dropbox, Zappos, and IBM are taking this notion seriously and the results show. Everyday companies are surging ahead in their markets by figuring out how to leverage diversity. They are leapfrogging ahead of those who simply tolerate differences. The research is overwhelming in support of the financial and social benefits of such leaders.

Diversity means conflict. Differences in appearance, perspectives, values, natural gifts, and experience can all set the stage for conflict. Compassion turns this conflict into opportunity. Drama uses it against people. Differences are seen as a threat or liability, something to be controlled or avoided. Historically, we've seen this manifested most clearly along the lines of race, gender, ethnicity, sexual orientation, and religion. It can also be seen with regards to character strengths.

Consider a person who is naturally gifted in being logical, responsible and organized. In the same spirit of the saying, "If all you have is a hammer, the whole world is a nail," this person runs the risk of thinking that logic and organization are the only best way to negotiate life at home and in the workplace. At work this person might think that everyone should work a regular schedule from eight to five, expect everyone to organize their office or cubicle in a certain way, and assume that everyone will be most productive by conforming to a certain routine. The prejudicial assumption running through his mind is, "if everyone would just do their job like me then we would not have any problems."

Under stress, this person may start to attack others who do not do the work as he does; making comments like, "What are they thinking," or, "The job would be easier if they would just do it like me." If this person is in a management position, he might label people who aren't like him as lazy, irresponsible, and stupid. He might fire them and hire only those who have qualities similar to him. This is when diversity is lost! People with different character strengths, different ways of getting the job done, different perspectives on problem-solving don't fit. The logical and data-driven person is prejudiced against those who have different strengths and negatively stereotypes them.

At home this same logical, responsible person in a parenting role might expect his child to show the same qualities. He might say to his daughter, "What were you thinking?" and call her an idiot when she makes a mistake. She might begin to believe, "Dad will only love me if I think like him. I don't fit in my own home." What if his daughter is a fun-loving, creative kid who likes to be with her friends and does not take life overly serious, still gets good grades, goes to school, and doesn't get into too much trouble?

By trying to make his daughter into a clone of himself, dad abuses diversity within his own family and the drama begins. Often the power struggles lead to negative behaviors. The parent falsely believes, "If only my child could think straight like me, she would turn out OK." Meanwhile his daughter says to herself, "My dad doesn't understand me and life is no fun anymore." This leads to numerous power struggles while the parent pushes his child away because he is unable to accept how she is wonderfully different.

In Drama, our own strengths can be used against us as well. The very same strengths that helped a person successfully negotiate differences and disagreements begin to be used negatively. For example, persons who are logical and data driven can become paralyzed by the unending need for more data. They are unable to make decisions for fear of missing something or not having a perfect answer. The gift of empathy and compassion can become distorted so that a person abandons her own needs and boundaries and burns out from compassion fatigue. The gift of persuasion, wonderfully manifested as charismatic leadership, becomes abused as manipulation and narcissism in the Drama Triangle.

Taibi Kahler, an author, advisor to a US president, consultant to NASA, and a gifted psychologist, has done outstanding research to map the highly predictable nature of distress, how gifts become liabilities, strengths become weaknesses, and how when in distress a person can exert increasingly futile effort while only digging a deeper hole for herself. More on this in upcoming chapters.

To see where you stand, ask a trusted friend or colleague to rate you on the following list of behaviors. Again, use the rating scale outlined earlier.

Leveraging Diversity (Compassion)	Misuse/Abuse of Diversity (Drama)
__ Can connect with many different kinds of people	__ Is unable to connect with people different from self
__ Is knowledgeable about the dimensions of diversity	__ Is ignorant or unaware of the many dimensions of diversity
__ Designs tasks and projects to utilize multiple different views and talents	__ Designs tasks and projects to use one or two gifts and talents
__ Celebrates different perspectives and approaches to problem solving	__ Discourages different perspectives and approaches to problem solving
__ Avoids putting people into boxes or categories	__ Quickly labels people or makes assumptions based on limited information
___ Leveraging Diversity % Average	___ Misuse/Abuse of Diversity % Average

Table 2: Checklist for Leveraging Diversity vs. Misusing/Abusing Diversity

Conflict that Creates vs. Conflict that Destroys

"Conflict is inevitable, but combat is optional."

—Max Lucado

Michael Meade, a poet, mythologist, musician and storyteller, suggests that the purpose of conflict is to create. This radical notion implies that conflict has a purpose, that it occurs because something new needs to be brought into a world that didn't know it needed it. Much like the conflict between sand and the oyster produces the pearl, conflict between people presents an opportunity to create new solutions.

The ability to engage in productive conflict is one of the marks of a great team and something we focus heavily on in our leadership development and team alignment work. Positive conflict involves passionate dialogue about issues and ideas without attacking the person behind the idea. In the Compassion Triangle, conflict is turned into opportunity in the following ways:

1. There are clear rules of engagement or behavioral norms for what's expected during positive conflict and what to do when the norms are violated.

2. There is a clear process for decision making and feedback so that people know what to expect.

3. There is accountability among team members for enforcing the rules of engagement.

These guidelines require the qualities of Persistence, Openness, and Resourcefulness. By contrast, Drama turns conflict into destruction. Victims avoid conflict and give up their own power in order to maintain harmony. Persecutors shut down healthy conflict by criticizing or attacking others for being stupid, lazy, or uncommitted. They can also become intolerant of conflict altogether and squash open dialogue. Rescuers attempt to sideline conflict by enabling inappropriate behaviors and relationships, thus preventing new solutions. In Drama, conflict perpetuates more conflict and reinforces negative relationships rather than stimulating new solutions and healthy relationships. The most frequent consequence is that endless time and resources are spent trying solutions that never get to the root of the problem. When people ask us, "How do we know if we are in drama as an organization?," we often ask them to look at their policy manual for the answer. Usually, the bigger the policy manual, the more drama is infecting the organization.

To find out how you approach conflict, ask a trusted colleague or friend to rate you on the following checklist of behaviors.

Creative Conflict (Compassion)	Destructive Conflict (Drama)
__ Encourages and supports overt rules of engagement to keep conflict safe	__ Supports unspoken rules of engagement that make conflict unsafe
__ Can engage in passionate dialogue about an idea and disagree without attacking	__ Disagreements degenerate into arguments and personal attacks
__ Supports a safe environment for everyone to participate and all sides of an issue to be heard	__ Conflict usually results in the same one or two people dominating the conversation
__ Expresses value for different perspectives and approaches	__ Criticizes or dismisses different points of view
__ Listens with curiosity to understand	__ Listens to defend one's own position or form a counter-argument
__ Creative Conflict % Average	__ Destructive Conflict % Average

Table 3: Checklist for Creative vs. Destructive Conflict

Collaboration vs. Competition

We've all grown up around competition. From math contests to youth sports, from sales contests to departmental fund-raisers, competition is everywhere and finds healthy outlets throughout our culture. When communication becomes competitive, however, we believe that everybody loses.

Let's explore how this plays out in the workplace. Jim has one perspective and Jo has another; each has what they believe to be a valid approach to solve a problem. Staying in the Compassion Triangle, they will collaborate. They will explore each other's perspective, listen to understand, be open to alternative solutions, leverage diversity, and likely find the best overall approach that serves the needs of their team or organization.

If, instead, they choose the drama path, they will see their differences in perspectives as a competition — a battle to be won or lost. Digging in heels, becoming defensive, caving in, forming camps, or discounting others are all signs that a person has taken a competitive stance in which someone must triumph and the other person goes down. Fueled by myths, each role in the Drama Triangle has a predictable approach to competition.

In Drama, the Persecutor plays to win at another's expense. He or she is invested in winning, and can become equally invested in the other person losing. Attacking opposing ideas, closed-minded thinking, tunnel vision, self-justification, criticism, blaming, sarcasm and insults all send the message "I am right, you are wrong," "I am committed, you are not," and "I am smart, you are dumb."

When a Persecutor insists that someone apologize or admit they were wrong, the competition is on. While they may appear righteous in their rationale that an apology is a sign of respect and accountability, the myth behind it is "I can make you feel bad emotionally."

You may be asking yourself, "Who on earth would tolerate and play along with this dastardly game of the Persecutor?" None other than the Victim, who is more than willing to accept defeat and play the role of the loser. Buying into their own myth that "You can make me feel bad emotionally," the Victim accepts the invitation into drama and allows the attacks of the Persecutor to go unchallenged.

And, finally, in this dismal game of win-lose, who will officiate? The Rescuer, of course. Wanting desperately to fix the problem, they mediate, give advice, enable, and divert the carnage because in drama, they believe the myth that "I can make you feel good emotionally." In our experience, many clients would like us to play the Rescuer role (and many consultants fall victim to this invitation), so that they can feel better without being accountable. They ask for advice, recommendations, and explanations, and would prefer we play the role of expert rather than holding them accountable for making substantive changes in their drama-based habits. We refuse to play this role. The inevitable result of trying to rescue your client is that they are looking for a new consultant next year. Hoping for a magic fix, they keep searching for and external answer to their suffering.

The personal and professional cost of competition in the Drama Triangle is significant. Problems don't get addressed, creative minds get shut down, people burn out, and relationships turn ugly. Research on employee retention and productivity shows that employees leave their leaders, not their companies. This is almost always due to drama. When supervisors or leaders operate out of drama, they broadcast strong invitations to all those around to jump on board and begin to spread negative competition. This is true even in parent-child relationships. Resentment, anger, and animosity start to set in. This sets the stage for teams to break down, factions to form, and rogue employees to begin controlling the work place.

The proverbial "analysis paralysis" in leadership teams is a consequence of competition in the Drama Triangle. One group works tirelessly to amass evidence, data, and projections to discern the best next step, while another group criticizes the new ideas or conclusions. A third group sits silent, and are just as responsible for the consequences.

Supervisors choose not to support a brilliant employee because they feel threatened by new ideas. Leadership teams spend thousands of dollars on outside consultants because they can't face the possibility that one of their own might have a "winning idea."

Competition in the Drama Triangle undermines effective decision making because it takes the focus off of what's best and on to what's going to help me feel justified. I've (Jeff) worked with divorcing couples who compete over time, money, and child support. In one situation a spouse actually spent more money on attorney fees than they would spend on child support. Top leaders spend money supporting a department that is losing money, only to intimidate another department they don't like.

Where are you at? Where's your team at? Complete the checklist below to find out your collaboration vs. competition ratio.

Collaborate (Compassion)	Compete (Drama)
__ Brings all ideas out on the table	__ Keeps pushing one's own idea over and over
__ Explores the pros and cons of all ideas	__ Focuses on the pros of my ideas and the cons of others' ideas
__ Looks for hybrid solutions	__ Is inflexible in blending solutions
__ Focuses on what's truly best for the team or organization	__ Rationalizes own agenda as "best for the team"
__ Looks for ways to use different skill sets	__ Looks for ways to use my skill set
___ Collaborate % Average	___ Compete % Average

Table 4: Checklist for for Collaboration vs. Competition

Empowerment vs. Control

"Rather than heroes who tell us what to do, we need servants who help us do the work ourselves."

—David Chrislip and Carl Larson

Empowerment is not about what we do *to* people, but about our attitude and approach *with* them. By definition, it is impossible to empower another person because it would be buying into the myth that "I can make you feel good emotionally."

However, we can facilitate the conditions to make it easier for people to empower themselves. All of the compassion skill sets described in this chapter work together to facilitate fertile conditions for empowerment. When effectiveness is the order of the day, people can make choices to participate in helpful ways. When perspective is present and when leaders are in touch with reality, it becomes safe to try new things and suggest different approaches. When diversity is being leveraged, it becomes an asset to bring unique gifts to the table. And when there are a forum and ground rules for productive conflict, people can reach for new heights.

By contrast, the collective impact of the drama-based approaches described in this chapter result in a control and fear-based environment. Fear and force have never been long-term solutions to productivity. Instead, they simply engender more fear and more force. Daniel Pink, in his book, *Drive*[3], shows compelling evidence that extrinsic motivation (control) simply doesn't work as a motivator in anything but the most rudimentary and routine tasks. Yet the desire to control people, things, the natural world, and even the future is part of being

---

3 Pink, D. (2005). *Drive: The Surprising Truth about What Motivates Us*. Penguin, New York, NY

human, particularly when we are under stress. The feeling of being out of control is frightening, and humans seek to avoid it when possible.

Justification seeks to believe that I have control over how things turn out for myself and others. Tunnel vision leads to a delusional sense of control over reality. Abuse of diversity oversimplifies the beautiful potential in people and attempts to predict behavior by reducing people to stereotypes. And, destructive conflict gives the illusion of control by resulting in the same outcomes over and over, even when those outcomes are clearly ineffective.

Where do you stand on the Empowerment to Control continuum? Complete the checklist below to find out your empowerment-to-control ratio. As before, rate by splitting 100 percent between the pair of Compassion and Drama statetments in each row.

Empowerment (Compassion)	Control (Drama)
__ Listen with curiosity, with a goal of understanding	__ Listen in order to respond, impatient to share what's on your mind
__ Invite others to expand on their visions and ideas	__ Speak for others, maybe even finish their sentences
__ Explore ways that others' gifts can help solve problems	__ Limit solutions to your areas of expertise or comfort
__ Ask for help when you need it	__ Don't ask for help when you need it
__ Support failing forward	__ Criticize failure, or rescue others from making their own mistakes
__ Seek ways to support intrinsic motivation and inspiration in others	__ Believe that fear or guilt are legitimate motivators
____ Empowerment % Average	____ Control % Average

Table 5: Checklist for Empowerment vs. Control

Seeking Connection vs. Seeking Exception

It's human nature to look for novelty. It's evolutionarily adaptive to notice what's out of place, particularly if it poses a threat or could indicate something isn't happening as it should. When it comes to dynamic relationships with others, this human tendency can backfire.

In drama, people focus on how others are different, look for what's wrong with others' ideas and perspectives, and become invested in seeking exception. Several classic phrases let you know that a person is seeking exception. "Playing devil's advocate" is one of my (Nate) favorites. As if this caveat somehow makes it OK to seek exception. Why not just say, "I disagree with you" in a respectful way?

The word *but* is another example of looking for exception. Many a great compliment and well-intended message has been erased by the word. "That's a great idea, but you missed a key element." A coaching client of mine (Nate) put it simply by stating, "Whenever you use the word *but*, you make whatever you just said a lie." You may as well have just saved your breath and started with "You missed a key element," because the receiver of your message won't remember the positives you offered. So often we observe team decision making processes where the first word out of someone's mouth is "but." What a great way to undermine whatever the other person said and broadcast that your agenda is all that matters. In case you are trying to find a loophole, the word *however* is no better; it's just *but* in a tuxedo.

A vivid contemporary example of seeking exception is the current political climate in the United States. One doesn't have to watch cable news networks for long to see that they are more invested in being against whatever the other political party is doing than providing meaningful news coverage. Drama is their formula for ratings. I (Nate) recently sent a relative of mine a financial analysis by Forbes Magazine outlining one perspective on how the current president was helping the economy. His response, "That just goes to show you that the media will say anything to support a failing president." I asked him what, specifically, he disagreed with in the article. His response, "I didn't read it." Seeking exception leads people to dismiss anything other than evidence to support their myths. In this instance, the myth is that "I'm OK, You're not OK."

"The heighth of wisdom is the ability to simultanously entertain opposing points of view."

—Plato

In Compassion, people seek connection. They seek to find synergy, add value, and build on others' contributions. They understand that rarely does one person have the only, best idea and that innovation comes from open dialogue that welcomes different points of view. We recommend replacing the word *but* with the word *and*. It may seem like a relatively innocuous shift, yet it can have profound consequences. Our clients regularly object to this, challenging us and seeking exception to this invitation. As we dig deeper, we find that the real shift isn't in the word. It's in what the word represents. To say, "That's a great idea, and I'd like to offer some additional thoughts" changes things considerably.

Plato is credited with defining wisdom as the ability to simultaneously entertain opposing points of view. Entertaining another view does not mean endorsing or acting on it. It simply means allowing apparent contradictions to coexist without judgment while possibility germinates. It's about allowing conflict to create. We invite you to replace *but* with *and*, experience how it enhances the respect you show to others, challenges your own ego, and opens up more productive dialogue. If your heart is seeking connection, your words and behaviors will follow.

People who seek connection delight in great solutions, no matter where they come from. They are willing to approach problem solving as a synergistic, evolutionary process where one person's contribution may spark another's idea, and together something wonderful emerges.

Seeking connection means taking the time and effort to understand another person's perspective. In doing so, you are able to make an informed choice about whether to help nurture an idea other than your own, take inspiration from it and take it to a new level, or be open about your disagreement or concern when appropriate. Seeking connection and leveraging diversity often go together in the Compassion Triangle. Seeking connection means looking for ways that each person's gifts can contribute to realizing innovative solutions. One of the best examples of seeking connection is the phenomenon of open source software, in which dozens, or even thousands of creative brains around the world seek to contribute, add value, and help build a better product. The end goal: add value to build a greater whole.

What is your ratio of seeking connection vs. seeking exception? To find out, complete these checklists using the same rating scale as before.

Seeking Connection (Compassion)	Seeking Exception (Drama)
__ Express appreciation for others people's input	__ Ignore, discount, or undermine others people's input
__ Use AND to build on another's ideas.	__ Use BUT to discount others and put your perspective first.
__ Help others explore the potential in their contributions.	__ Play devil's advocate.
__ Delight in great ideas, regardless of where they come from.	__ Feel threatened by solutions other than your own.
__ Entertain opposing points of view without judgment.	__ Dismiss opposing points of view.
__ Seeking Connection % Average	__ Seeking Exception % Average

Table 6: Checklist for for Seeking Connection vs. Seeking Exception

Taken together, the dynamics of the compassion-drama continuum offer a granular assessment of where you currently are and how those around you are coping. Table 7 offers a summary of the nine dynamics along with a place for you to enter your scores from each one, using the same scoring system as before. We encourage you to complete this page and use it with your employees, peers, or team. Discover where you are, and set goals using the target behaviors from the Compassion side of each checklist. Or, try out our online Drama Assessment at drama.next-element.com.

Compassion	Score	Score	Drama
Perspective			Tunnel-Vision
Effective			Justified
Realistic			Delusional
Forward Failing			Backward Failing
Leveraging Diversity			Misuse/Abuse Diversity
Creative Conflict			Destructive Conflict
Collaborate			Compete
Empowerment			Control
Seeking Connection			Seeking Exception

Table 7: Summary of Drama-Compassion Dimensions

In the next chapter, we'll go behind the scenes to explain why people enter Drama in the first place, and what you can do about it.

CHAPTER 8

May I Have Your Attention, Please?

Humans need attention. Period. By attention, we mean those in-born hungers that get each of us up each day to do what we do. It's what bakes our cake, floats our boat, rings our bell, fills our tank. It's the psychological oxygen that fuels our engine.

What are the needs that drive human behavior? Much work has been done on the nature of human motivation. From Freud's psychosexual stages to Maslow's hierarchy of needs to McClelland's achievement, affiliation, and power needs, researchers have attempted to define, measure, and predict what makes us tick. Entire systems of management, leadership, and counseling have been built around models of motivation.

Understanding motivation is the next step in mapping the course from drama to compassion. In Chapters 6 and 7 we examined the dynamics of drama and their compassionate counterparts. In this chapter we will show how motivation, attention, human drive — whatever you want to call it — plays a critical role in both drama and compassion. By gaining precision and proficiency in motivating ourselves and others, we can spend less time in drama and more time in compassionate interactions.

The Uniqueness of Human Motivation

Not all people are motivated in the same way. The best teachers, leaders, mentors, and parents are those who are able to individualize approaches based on unique personal motivators to "meet people where they're at." Some people seem to be naturals at this while others find it very challenging. Most of us are somewhere in between, able to motivate some types of people better than others.

Is there a secret to motivating people? What do the best communicators and motivators know that the rest of us don't? According to the work of Daniel Goleman[1] and other leadership experts, these people both understand human motivation and have a deep desire to inspire others. They develop and practice the compassion skills of Openness, Resourcefulness, and Persistence.

The Process Communication Model

Let's get specific. What are the core drivers of human behavior? To answer this question, we look again to Dr. Taibi Kahler's Process Communication Model® (PCM). Our opinion is that PCM is the most comprehensive, inclusive, descriptive, elegant, and applicable model of human communication and motivation currently available. Trained in Transactional Analysis and recipient of the 1977 Eric Berne Memorial Scientific Award, Dr. Kahler was keenly interested in how the way people communicate correlates with personality.

Kahler's model focuses on process instead of content and offers a methodology for understanding the "how" of communication. In Chapter 1, we mentioned Randy Olson's book, *Don't Be Such a Scientist*, to illustrate the importance of style as well as substance. PCM takes this one step further by outlining scientifically-proven behavioral strategies

---

1 Goleman, G. (2006). *Social intelligence: The New Science of Human Relationships.* Bantam, New York, NY

for tailoring the process, or style, of our messages to reach each person with whom we communicate. PCM is a multidimensional model that has wide-ranging applications for communication, engagement, and motivation, as well as organizational development and strategy.

An online assessment determines a person's communication preferences and personality structure, including the ordering and relative strength of six different personality types within each of us. For example, one of the six Kahler Types, the Harmonizer, experiences the world through their emotions, preferring to share feelings with others, prizing friendship and relationships. Harmonizers are motivated by knowing that they are valued as a person, no strings attached. Using results from the Personality Pattern Inventory (PPI), individuals and teams can proceed with a variety of interpretive and skill-building formats to help develop self-awareness, communication, motivation, and conflict resolution.

PCM is a comprehensive model for understanding differences between people, why they do what they do, and how to work with them most effectively. In short, it is a framework for leveraging diversity by attending to process. Unlike other models of personality, PCM teaches skills to attend to process by interpreting the meaning of behaviors (words, tones, postures, gestures, and facial expressions) second by second, determine whether miscommunication is occurring, and intervene with precision to invite more healthy communication.

Among its numerous applications, PCM has been used by Fortune 500 companies to improve leadership communication, at NASA to screen and coach astronauts for the space shuttle program, and in gubernatorial and presidential campaigns to win elections. It has been utilized in education to improve academic outcomes while reducing behavior problems in the classroom, in psychotherapy to improve treatment outcomes, in filmmaking to craft more compelling characters and story lines, in marketing to reach more customers, and in a variety of personal settings from parenting to mentoring to volunteer management.

PCM outlines eight psychological needs that drive behavior: Time Structure, Recognition of Work, Recognition of Conviction, Recognition of Person, Sensory, Solitude, Contact, and Incidence. These needs are like oxygen, a necessary condition for productive functioning. Kahler has correlated these needs with specific personality types. We value and motivate people when we appreciate (Open) these needs in ourselves and others, assist (Resourceful) each other in feeding these needs in healthy ways, and leverage (Persistent) these needs towards common goals. Let's look at each one in detail.

Time Structure

Some people have an inborn need to structure and keep track of time. Time is a precious commodity that gives meaning, purpose, and direction to their lives. "What time is it?," "How much time do we have?," and "What time do you want the project completed?" are typical questions asked by persons with time structure needs. Clocks, calendars, and agendas all help meet these needs. These persons are motivated when they know the time elements of a task, such as when it's due or when to start. We honor time structure needs when we pay attention to time and when we allow and assist persons in structuring their time.

Getting needs met is both a personal responsibility and a gift we give others. Each of us is responsible to get our needs met in healthy ways. At the same time, we can choose to be responsible to our friends, family, and colleagues by appreciating, assisting, and leveraging their needs.

Examples of taking personal responsibility to get positive time structure needs met:
- using a planner or calendar
- scheduling important activities
- making a personal agenda

Examples of honoring another's time structure needs:
- being on time
- providing clarity and predictability around project time frames
- recognizing the importance of their time:
"Thanks for being on time," "Your time is important,"
"Do you have time?"

Recognition of Work

Accomplishment and achievement is immensely rewarding for some people. Whether organizing ideas into a coherent flow, arranging tasks in a more efficient way, or checking things off a list, people who need recognition for their work are most productive when their accomplishments are appreciated. Recognizing their ability and desire to plan, arrange, and execute tasks and ideas is how we value and motivate them. Recognition does not have to mean being in the limelight, big ceremonies, or fancy awards. It simply refers to where we focus attention. For individuals with the need for work recognition, noticing their efficient work and organized ideas is the most important way to motivate them.

Examples of taking personal responsibility to get positive recognition for work needs met:
- make lists and check them off when tasks are completed
- schedule time to celebrate accomplishments
- keep a journal of personal work accomplishments

- set goals and work towards them
- ask a trusted friend, peer, or supervisor to look at work you've done

Examples of honoring another's recognition for work needs:
- acknowledge and appreciate their hard work
- ask for their ideas
- support goal-setting and planning
- provide clear parameters and unambiguous feedback about work performance

Recognition of Conviction

"If a job is worth doing, it's worth doing well." If you've ever uttered these words, then you might have a need for recognition of conviction. For some people, their behavior flows from their convictions. Persons with this need take great care forming, discerning, and living their values. Recognition of conviction means respecting that a person has guiding beliefs and uses them as their compass for making choices.

Examples of taking personal responsibility to recognize convictions:
- ask for permission, then share your values and beliefs with others
- support a cause in your community in which you believe
- join a civic organization, board, or advocacy group
- make a personal mission statement

Examples of honoring another's need to have convictions recognized:
- respect their values, even if you don't agree with them
- acknowledge their commitment and dedication
- recognize their loyalty, perseverance, and courage
- learn about what's important to them
- ask about their guiding values

Recognition of Person

Recognition of person is the unconditional love and acceptance of another person for who they are. No strings attached. Sharing feelings, being vulnerable and open in an emotionally safe environment, and relishing relationships are ways that personhood is recognized. Phrases such as "You are special," "You are so thoughtful," and "I appreciate you being here" are some examples of how to offer recognition of person. While these persons are capable of working hard, being loyal, and thinking clearly, they operate from the motto, "I don't care how much you know until I know how much you care." Concern, empathy, close relationships, and sense of community are the hallmarks of recognition of person.

Examples of taking personal responsibility for recognition of person:
- make positive self-statements that you are unconditionally lovable
- share your feelings with loved ones
- enjoy close relationships where you feel valued unconditionally
- post pictures of persons whom you love and who care about you
- ask for what you want to feel safe and comfortable

Examples of honoring another's need for recognition of person:
- Take an interest in their family and friendships
- Tell them you appreciate them
- Look them in the eye and smile
- Empathize with their feelings
- Allow appropriate touch, such as a hug
- Spend time just being together

Sensory

Persons with sensory needs are highly attuned to how things taste, smell, feel, sound, and look. Sensory stimulation is an important source of motivation for them. These needs are met when they take care to surround themselves with pleasing, comfortable, enjoyable, and nurturing sensory experiences.

Examples of taking personal responsibility for sensory needs:
- enjoy a tasty meal in a pleasing environment
- use makeup, clothes, and jewelry that look nice and feel good
- get a massage, enjoy a soft blanket or other comforting activities
- surround yourself with music, smells, and sights that nurture you

Examples of honoring another's sensory needs:
- compliment jewelry, haircut, or clothing choices
- give gifts of flowers, food, and other things that appeal to the senses
- tend to creature comforts, such as room lighting or a comfortable chair

Contact

The need for contact involves physical, emotional, and playful contact with things and people. Whether bantering with colleagues, playing a game, listening to music, or creating something novel, contact needs are being met whenever a person is bouncing off of and reacting to the world around her. Free expression is a hallmark of this motivational need. Persons getting their contact needs met are sometimes judged by others as unprofessional, disrespectful, or juvenile. Contact can be obtained in negative ways, which often gives these people a bad rap.

The good news is that contact needs can be met in many appropriate ways.

Examples of taking personal responsibility for contact needs:
- express yourself creatively through art, music, dance, and other projects
- get physical through exercise, dance, and other forms of movement
- play games whenever you can
- tell jokes when appropriate
- listen to music
- find toys and games that are stimulating and fun

Examples of honoring another's contact needs:
- tell jokes and listen to their jokes
- give high fives, bumps, and other physical contact
- allow space and time for play
- avoid imposing excessive restrictions and rules
- support spontaneity whenever possible

Solitude

For some, simply being alone with no agenda or expectations is motivating and rejuvenating. Many who believe they need solitude simply want time without distractions to work, think, plan, complete tasks, or brainstorm. Solitude is different. It is the creation of open space and time where the mind can wander while opening up to imagination. Here's an anonymous quote that captures the essence of solitude: "Imagination comes, works, when you are not trying, when you have a peculiar, passive clarity." Solitude might be found in activities such as meditation, wandering alone in a park, sailing, yoga, or playing an instrument.

Examples of taking personal responsibility for getting solitude needs met:
- give yourself permission to take time for yourself without expectations to get anything particular done
- get into nature, away from people
- turn off the phone, tablet, and computer for a while
- build alone-time into your schedule

Examples of honoring another's solitude needs:
- avoid the urge to include them in every social activity
- give them adequate time and space to reflect and ponder
- don't push them to answer questions on the spot or participate in brainstorming
- give them advance notice if you want their input on something
- give them direct and discrete commands about what you want them to do and then leave them alone

Incidence

Kahler defines incidence as "a great deal of action in a short period of time." Persons with need for incidence are motivated by the unexpected, competition, excitement, challenge, thrill of the chase, adrenaline and immediate rewards. Inside, they are asking themselves, "Will I be able to pull it off?" Procrastination is often a strategy to increase incidence because it raises the stakes. Activities such as gambling, racing, competitive sports, public speaking, sales, and entrepreneurial ventures fill this need.

Examples of taking personal responsibility for healthy incidence:
- enter a competition
- start a small business venture
- volunteer to lead a fundraiser or promote a product
- procrastinate just long enough to add some excitement

Examples of honoring another's need for Incidence:
- dare them to do something productive and healthy
- make a deal with them, engage in negotiation
- put them in charge of something unique or special
- turn a normal task into a healthy competition, even a race against the clock
- if appropriate, offer immediate rewards, monetary or otherwise
- give them a little limelight

There you have it, the eight psychological needs that motivate human beings. No single need is more or less important, better or worse. The most important lesson here is that people are motivated differently, and that by meeting psychological needs, we unlock our best selves to reach our highest potential.

Now that we've examined the core drivers of human behavior, let's take a look at why we should care or act on this knowledge.[2]

---

2 PocketPCM smart phone app offers convenient reference guide PCM concepts and strategies, including motivational needs, in several languages. Available for Apple and Android operating systems.

SECTION THREE

The Toolkit

CHAPTER 9

Becoming an Effective Motivator

Have you ever been in your element, in an environment where things just seemed to flow effortlessly and were completely engrossed in whatever you were doing, feeling successful and worthwhile? In these situations, I'll bet that you were fully motivated, meeting your motivational needs in positive and productive ways and doing what you do best. Attending to our motivational needs allow us to mobilize our best selves, operate at our peak capacity, and utilize our natural gifts and abilities.

Positive attention, the right flavor of positive attention, is the key to unlocking our potential. Here are three steps in maximizing this potential and spending more time in the compassion triangle.

Step 1: Become Aware (Openness)

The first step is awareness and understanding of our own and others' unique psychological needs. This can be done by paying close attention, watching for behavior patterns, listening closely to others when they describe their ideal work environments or relationships, and reflecting on times when people functioned at their best. We invite you to look for the patterns we've described in the previous chapter. See if you can figure out how you and the important people in your life are motivated. Awareness is the first step.

Step 2: Learn New Skills (Resourcefulness)

Step 2 is learning how to authentically value different people by offering each one the motivation they respond to best. This is easier said than done. Each of us is partial to our own motivators, and we will naturally offer those to others. If recognition of time structure is important to me, I am likely to unconsciously and authentically offer it to others. If contact is important to me, I might find myself naturally finding the light side in conversations. After all, isn't this what the Golden Rule teaches? Doing what comes naturally is easy and self-motivating. Unfortunately, as a strategy for motivating others, it's hit and miss.

We've seen many well-intentioned parents, supervisors, pastors, and executives offer truckloads of their own favorite motivators, only to see performance and morale mysteriously decline. Not knowing the cause and making assumptions from their own perspective, they mistakenly assume that quantity is the problem. Redoubling their efforts, they add fuel to the fire and can easily become jaded or assume that their children, employees, or spouses are lazy and unmotivated. The irony is that they are partially correct. The person is indeed unmotivated. What is also true that they cannot see is that they are partially responsible for the problem. They are limited by tunnel vision, which leads to self-justification.

Right about now, you may be saying to yourself, "It's not authentic to change my style for others. That feels fake. I'd rather be true to myself than try to please everyone around me. This is just another manipulation strategy." We hear this often, mostly from persons who are motivated by recognition of work and conviction. For them, life is about being honest, consistent, and true to one's values. Individualizing how one interacts with others feels shifty and inauthentic.

If you share this concern, we offer several perspectives that may help. Let's begin with a paraphrased quote by Virginia Satir, noted American author and psychotherapist:

"The success of your communication is the response you get. If you don't get the response you want, change the way you communicate."

— Virginia Satir

Satir unveils the paradoxical selfishness inherent in sticking to your guns. Effective communication is not about you, it's about the other person. Effective motivators honor and respect others by adjusting to meet their needs. Humility and respect mean making the needs of others important, too. From this perspective, individualizing how we communicate and motivate others is a way of showing respect and building trust. Choosing not to adjust your style, even when you know the other person needs it, is selfish.

Another perspective has to do with habits and comfort. Doing what comes naturally feels right, and it is a habit. What comes naturally is what comes easily. Staying in your favorite and comfortable place isn't that hard. Reaching out to others on their terms takes effort, particularly if it requires developing new skills.

Finally, consider the dynamic of Effective vs. Justified. Being authentic by sticking to your own preferred style certainly can help you feel justified. But the key question is: How effective are you at motivating others? If you feel justified, i.e. "right," but are not being effective, it's time to look in the mirror.

"Do unto others as they'd have you do unto them."

- Platinum Rule

Valuing people according to their needs is what we call the Platinum Rule: "Do unto others as they'd have you do unto them." This requires a new skill set, the ability to reach out to others in their preferred style — the style that fills their tank and boosts their natural energy. This requires leaving our own comfort zone, challenging our own assumptions about what works, and putting the other person first. We contend that people can do this and maintain their own sense of identity and values. Everyday our clients find new levels of effectiveness while remaining true to themselves. Many describe it as growing more fully into their own potential. Some invoke a spiritual perspective, arguing that we all have within us a part of "the other" and when we connect fully with ourselves we are able to connect more fully with others.

To practice step 2, we recommend that you imagine how you might approach a person differently now that you understand how he is motivated. How might you value him? Maybe saying "good job" [recognition of work] isn't the right compliment. Maybe "I appreciate you" [recognition of person] is what he really wants to hear.

If you are a parent, imagine how you might set up homework, dinner time, or trips to the grocery store in a way that naturally motivates your child. If your child is motivated by playful contact, a boring dinner routine is a recipe for trouble. Maybe music or games will help the peas go down. If your child is motivated by time structure, then use lists and agendas to help them organize their time and clean their room.

At work, imagine how you might set up reward systems, work environments, incentives, or annual job evaluations in a way that intrinsically motivates employees according to their individual needs. Don't be afraid to treat people differently. One of the biggest myths of effective work environments is that people should all be treated the same, aka fairly. This is a great recipe for mediocre performance. The Platinum Rule extends beyond equity. It is about justice, respect, dignity, and inspiration. People who are motivated according to their own needs don't complain or compare nearly as much as people who aren't motivated.

Step 3: Implement New Learning (Persistence)

Step 3 is about putting into practice what you've imagined and analyzed in step 2. It is about courageously acting on your intentions and plans. Don't be afraid to start small, experiment with these new tools, and see what happens. What do you have to lose? Begin with the things you have imagined in step 2, try them out, and see how they work. Maybe you've decided to offer more Recognition of Conviction to your boss. What are you going to say and when? Try it. See how it works. Try it again and get better. The great thing about motivation is that you know immediately if it's working. People who are motivated work harder and feel happier. Also, don't be afraid to ask people how they are best motivated or seek feedback after you've tried something new. If implementing the concepts in this chapter leads you to break out of a rut, expect a mixture of surprise, joy, and even skepticism from those who know you. Becoming more effective is a change, and people may not know what you're up to. Don't let that deter you. Finally, when you're working to be more effective, it's OK to make mistakes, to fail forward. It's an opportunity to learn what works and what doesn't.

"The great thing about trying is that there are only two outcomes. You can succeed. Or you can learn."

—Jim Korroch

Finally, don't give up. Be persistent. It takes time to develop new skills. You'll get better and better the more you practice. And remember, nothing breeds success like success. If you are intentional and use the concepts in this chapter, you can expect people around you to be more enthusiastic, engaged, trusting, and energized.

Before You Go Forth and Motivate

It's worth noting that some needs may be difficult to meet in certain environments. It's foolish and naive to believe that everyone can get their needs met all the time. For example, it may benefit me to subdue my need for contact when I am first meeting the CEO of my hottest prospect. It may be best to put my need for time structure on the back burner when my wife is putting the final touches on her makeup before we go out for dinner. It just might be best in the long run if I put my need for incidence temporarily on hold while I contemplate the consequences of sending that incendiary e-mail at 1:00 a.m. If psychological needs are our oxygen, then holding our breath is tolerable once in a while, for a short period of time. In certain moments, it's the most effective thing to do.

One of the great qualities of humans is that we have the ability to put our needs on hold temporarily in the interest of relationships, business, safety, and the future. This only becomes a problem when it becomes chronic, causes us to lose our energy, feel resentment, become depressed, explode in anger or engage in other inappropriate behavior. Caring elegantly for our own needs in appropriate ways allows us to make the healthy choice to reach out to others as well, to stay in the Compassion Triangle.

Cultural dynamics play a significant role in meeting psychological needs. We've discovered that certain cultures, even entire generations, have developed around certain psychological needs. For example, persons growing up in the Great Depression placed a high value on recognition of work, time structure, and convictions. You don't have to be around the Veteran generation for long to hear the messages of thrift, delayed gratification, prudence, trust, and perseverance. Generation Y is all about mobility, opportunity, individual expression, fun and excitement. The needs for incidence, contact, and recognition of person are much more central to our current Western culture than they were even 20 years ago. The African cultures in which I (Nate) grew up valued respect for elders, integrity, tradition, privacy, and honor. Recognition of conviction was highly valued in that culture. Eastern cultures like India, China, and Singapore are producing high numbers of excellent engineers, architects, and computer programmers. Recognition of work and time structure is highly valued in these cultures.

There's another side to the cultural or generational emphasis on certain needs. Life conditions change, and our world is a different place than it used to be. Certain qualities and skills are more adaptive and facilitative than they used to be. Consequently, we expect there to be shifts in environmental motivators that draw out those skills and gifts.

Is this a good thing? We aren't sure. What we do know is that when families, organizations, cultures, and even countries value certain motivators over others, something is lost. People get left behind. Gifts go unused. Potential gets wasted. Prejudice creeps in. We believe that in every family or organization there is a place for the beautiful diversity of gifts within people. We predict, therefore, that the most successful groups of the future will be those who know how to offer ways to meet all of the motivational needs.

Negative Attention is Better Than No Attention at All

Beyond the feel-good reasons to pay attention to unique human motivators, why is this so important? Why should we work so hard to understand motivation and adjust our behavior accordingly? Because there are significant and predictable consequences when we don't.

The Drama Triangle is all about the emotional distress dynamics that transpire when humans don't get their psychological needs met in healthy ways. Emotional (psychological) distress is most easily explained by a simple human phenomenon: negative attention is better than no attention at all. This transcends gender, ethnicity, race, and religion. Kahler's research on motivation also discovered that if we do not get our personality-based psychological needs met positively, we will find a way, consciously or unconsciously, to get those very same needs met negatively. This leads to predictable patterns of behavior in distress.[1] The reverse is also true: positively meeting our psychological needs is the most effective ways to get out of distress and stop the drama.

What does negative attention look like? Table 1 lists each psychological need, outlines its negative attention counterpart, and shows the corresponding Drama role.

Positive Need	Negative Attention Counterpart	Drama Role
Time Structure	Becomes preoccupied and obsessive around time, money, fairness, and equity. Unknowingly wastes everyone's time by micromanaging and over-controlling.	Persecutor
Recognition of Work	Attacks others for not working hard enough or smart enough. Micromanages, over-controls and criticizes others' work and ideas.	Persecutor

1 The Drama Triangle is descriptive of the general dynamics of drama. Kahler's research added predictive utility by showing how individual personality correlates with different levels of distress behavior, the unmet psychological needs behind the behavior, and corresponding roles on the Drama Triangle.

Positive Need	Negative Attention Counterpart	Drama Role
Recognition of Conviction	Pushes beliefs on others, crusades for or against causes, becomes self-righteous, opinionated and judgmental, engages in black-or-white thinking, is suspicious of others who don't believe the same.	Persecutor
Recognition of Person	Makes mistakes and inadvertently invites criticism, loses confidence, puts self down, sets self up to get rejected.	Victim
Sensory	Stops taking care of themselves, lets plants die, neglects pets.	Victim
Contact	Blames and is blameless, argumentative, negatively sarcastic, which leads to getting censured.	Persecutor
Solitude	Withdraws, avoids people, isolates, does not seek out direction or guidance, feels inadequate.	Victim
Incidence	Takes unhealthy or unsafe risks, manipulates, triangulates, sets up negative drama by stirring the pot and breaking rules.	Persecutor

Table 1: Positive Psychological Needs, Negative Attention Counterparts, and Drama Roles

Remember that how people get negative attention is predicted by their positive psychological needs. They are two sides of the same coin.

Table 1 paints a depressing picture. The sad truth is that efforts to get positive psychological needs met negatively account for most of the unhealthy interactions, strained relationships, fractured teams, and international conflicts in our world. This is human nature. Remember, *when people don't get their psychological needs met positively, they are driven to get those very same needs met negatively, with or without awareness.* It's not a matter of *if,* but a matter of *when* and how severe the damage will be. These patterns are amazingly consistent and predictable. The more time we spend in the Drama Triangle getting our needs met negatively and feeling justified while we are doing it, the harder it is to get out.

You may have noticed that when engaging in negative attention behavior, humans play either the Victim or Persecutor role. Thus, it is always a win – lose scenario. Persecutors are invested in winning while Victims are invested in losing. Conducting business, parenting, or relationships while seeking negative attention is always a win – lose proposition.

You may be asking: Why isn't the Rescuer mentioned here? It's such a critical role in Drama and we know plenty of people who go there. The answer lies in the severity of distress. The Rescuer role is played by some personality types in mild levels of distress as they are just hopping on to the Drama Triangle tilt-a-whirl.[2] Ultimately destined to fail in their efforts to save others, Rescuers often switch to Persecutors in deeper distress. We've all experienced the well-meaning supervisor, teacher, or friend who, when unsuccessful in trying to fix us, switches into attack mode with comments such as: "You wouldn't listen to me so you deserve what's coming to you," or "I tried, and you were too stubborn to take my advice," or "OK, fine. I'm done trying to help you." So, when the chips are down and the drama is severe enough, everyone plays the role of either a Victim or Persecutor.

The good news is that there's hope. Positively meeting our own and others' psychological needs is the best way to get out of distress and strop the drama. We encourage you to understand your own and others' unique psychological needs, develop the skills to get them met in healthy ways on a regular basis, and then make those skills a part of your daily habits of self-care.

---

2 For detailed description of distress dynamics and degrees of distress, see Kahler's book, *Process Therapy Model.*

CHAPTER 10

Expectations: The Double-Edged Sword

"An expectation is a resentment waiting to happen."

— Jon Carroll

Most of us accept that people are built and motivated differently. And, it probably comes as no surprise that humans get negative attention in ways that undermine productivity and relationships. Now, let's take a look at what this means for leadership, parenting, productivity, and relationships at all levels.

Expectations are a double-edged sword because they can be wielded as both content and process weapons. Failure to distinguish between the two leads to all sorts of negative consequences. In this chapter, we will explore expectations and see what they can teach us about the relationship between process, content, drama, compassion, and motivational needs.

Let's look first at the content application of the word expectation. Expectations are standards, goals, or defined end states of behavior. "We have high expectations for ourselves" is a way of saying that our standards are high. "Setting realistic expectations" means to set goals that are achievable. Used in this way, expectations are the content, simply a way to describe what we want to achieve.

Projecting Motivational Needs

Looking back on motivational needs, we can see that expectations as content might be quite motivating for those whose psychological needs are recognition of work, time structure, and conviction. Each of these needs can lend themselves to goal setting, achievement, and accomplishment of a future end state. Simply setting a goal can be quite motivating. This is both a blessing and a curse. For persons who are intrinsically and internally motivated by content expectations, it may be very difficult to understand the difference between content (goal) and process (how I am uniquely and personally motivated to move towards that goal).

When expectation is used as process, the message between the lines is that someone is obligated to do something. Consider these statements: "I expect you to clean your room," "I expect you to complete your work by lunch," "I expect you to come to the team meeting on time," or "I expect you to stay out of trouble." In these examples, the communicator has unknowingly made the assumption that simply stating an expectation will somehow achieve the goal. Another way to explain what has happened is that one person's motivators are projected onto another person.

I'll illustrate with a real-life lesson that I (Jeff) learned very early on with my son and his desire to excel at basketball.

My need for recognition of conviction is illustrated by my philosophy that "If a job is worth doing, it's worth doing right." For some people, behavior flows from their convictions, beliefs, and values. Persons with this need are deeply intentional in forming, discerning, and living their values and listening to their consciences. Recognition of conviction means respecting and acknowledging that a person knows what they believe in and uses it as their compass for making choices.

My son, by contrast, is primarily motivated by physical, emotional, and playful contact with things and people. Whether bantering with his peers, playing a pickup basketball game, listening to music, or creating something novel, contact needs are being met whenever he is bouncing off and reacting to the world around him.

From the age of seven, my son stated that he liked basketball and that he would like to be good at it. My conviction needs kicked in and I began preaching, "If a job is worth doing, it's worth doing right." Translation: "If you are going to be good at basketball, then you must practice and here is how you should practice in order to be good."

Have you ever made that error in assuming that your own motivational needs will work for someone else? My son's primary need was for contact, which meant that basketball practice had to be fun and without too much structure. He wasn't unwilling or incapable of putting in the necessary work and practice to get better. But to keep his energy up, he had to have fun along the way. From my motivational perspective, I assumed that the value and end goal of being a good basketball player was sufficient to motivate him. It certainly motivated me to get involved! And, it motivates millions of parents every day to invest large amounts of money and time in their children.

At first it seemed that all our power struggles revolved around how he would practice basketball (process), not whether or not he wanted to play and be good (content). Each of us predictably ended up on the Drama Triangle, me angry and frustrated (Persecutor), him blaming me for everything and being oppositional (Persecutor). Both of us felt justified that we had it right and the other one was wrong. As long as I continued projecting my own motivational need onto my son, I continued to have negative responses when he didn't do as I wanted. And, I found myself deep into the myth behind the Persecutor Role: "I can make you feel bad emotionally to get you to do what I want." I was unable to see that my approach was getting us further away from both of our goals. I could not see that the goal itself was distinctly different from the process of how each of us could best move towards that goal.

When I gained awareness about his process and accepted him and his need for contact, we interacted much better. When we went to the gym we had fun, joked, and played. The direct impact of me changing and accepting him was that he worked harder in his own way, not mine. He was the able to set and accomplish his own goals, not my goals for him. In my current role as Head of school at the MUSE school, I frequently tell this story when I am conducting parent classes, parent tours, and interviews. I share with parents that one of the most difficult obstacles to overcome in education is to invite parents not to push their process agenda on their children, but to stop having process expectations.

Some of the most intractable power struggles arise when two people both compete for the Persecutor role on the Drama Triangle. Going back to the last chapter, recall that both Contact and Conviction needs are obtained negatively from the Persecutor role. It's as though both parties are playing to win at the other's expense. It is simply not sustainable without significant collateral damage. For my son and me, the power struggle created continual conflict and mutual resentment, damaging our relationship.

Wants vs. Expectations

In an effort to spend more time in the Compassion Triangle with my son, I have begun to replace expectations with wants. This helps me avoid projecting my motivational needs onto him. Instead of saying, "I expect you to do it like this," I now say, "I want you to practice and you can choose the way in which you practice. I will support your (process) style of practice." Let's break down these statements:

"I want you to practice." (Openness) I am honest about my desires, owning that they are my desires, not his.

"You can choose the way in which you practice." (Resourcefulness) I acknowledge that there may be multiple effective ways to get to the end goal. I realize that my process will only be beneficial to my son if he is open to it and that I cannot empower or control him. I can only support an environment in which he is most likely to take ownership over his behavior.

"I will support your style of practice." (Persistence) I will not give up on my son, nor will I take over for him or take responsibility for the consequences of his choices.

Being responsible *to* others *for* our behavior suggests we stay in the Compassion Triangle when boundaries have been crossed or people aren't doing as we would want them to. Staying open, persistent, and resourceful with others helps us avoid power struggles and be more effective. As soon as I let go of my expectations of my son's basketball methods (process), he performed much, much better. I don't know if he is the next Lebron James. However, as I write this, he is being recruited by several colleges to play basketball. He continues to love the sport and spends many hours a week practicing. Keeping clear about the difference between wants and expectations has transformed my relationship with my son. I have let go of expectation and replaced it by owning my wants. I focus on being open, resourceful, and persistent. He accomplishes what he wants to accomplish in a way that works best for him.

Wanting instead of expecting has transformed how my wife and I (Jeff) approach parenting. We want our children to be responsible. We want them to be successful. We want them to take ownership of their behavior. By staying in the Compassion Triangle, we have been able to eliminate many of the power struggles that are so often a part of child raising. Another example might help illustrate. Once our children reach the age ten, we do not have prescribed bedtimes. My wife and I have no expectations about when our children go to bed. Do we want our kids to be rested and make it to school every day? Absolutely. And we want them to find their own way to take ownership of the behaviors and attitudes that help them be successful. Guess what? Our kids have established their bedtime schedules and make good grades at school, without the burden of our expectation. They are learning how to listen to and respect their bodies, take care of themselves, and take ownership of the consequences of their actions.

It didn't happen overnight. There were those sleepy days following a 1:00 a.m. bedtime. There were those late notices at school because my son didn't wake up on time. We were tempted to jump into the Drama Triangle and say things like, "See, I told you this would happen" (Persecutor), wake them up and give them advice on how to manage their time better (Rescuer), or take them to school late while apologizing to the teacher for our terrible parenting and making ourselves late to work (Victim). Instead, we stuck to our promise of letting them discover the consequences of their choices without attacking them (Persistent), supporting them emotionally when they were suffering (Open), and assisting them in problem solving when they asked for help (Resourceful).

My wife and I (Nate) use the Compassion Triangle every day to enforce boundaries and help our children develop healthy habits. My oldest daughter's relationship with her cell phone is one example. Our policy is that she is limited to 2,000 texts per month on our family cell phone plan. If she goes over, she loses her phone for the rest of the billing cycle. Once in a great while she exceeds her limit, often leaving her unable to text with her friends, teammates, coach, and boyfriend. The following interaction illustrates my daughter's invitations into drama and how I respond compassionately without expectations.

Daughter: "Dad, I don't know what I'll do without my phone. My boyfriend will be mad at me if I don't respond to his texts." (Victim)

Dad: "I understand how hard it is to feel out of touch with your boyfriend (Open). If you'd like any help in problem solving how you are going to cope for the next week, I am happy to help (Resourceful). Our policy is unchanged from previous months, and you went over your limit so I am going to take your phone." (Persistent)

Daughter: "Dad, you are so mean! No other parents have such rigid rules. It's not fair and you're just being unreasonable." (Persecutor)

Dad: "I understand that you are angry. I remember once when I was grounded and couldn't call my friends on the phone. It was super embarrassing and I felt out of touch (Open). As I said, I'm happy to help you problem-solve this situation (Resourceful). And, I will take your phone away before you go to bed tonight." (Persistent)

Daughter: "It's just hard because this weekend is the back to school dance and everyone is going to be texting each other about what they are wearing (Open). May I text my boyfriend and friends really quick to let them know to call me on the phone if they need to reach me?" (Resourceful)

Dad: "Sure. (Open). Take your time. (Resourceful). I'll be back in a few minutes to get your phone." (Persistent)

Daughter: "OK (Persistent). Thanks, Dad." (Open)

Each time my daughter played a drama role, I responded with compassion by staying open, resourceful, and persistent. Sometimes it takes a few more trips around the Compassion Triangle, but this process is extremely effective in a variety of situations. If at any time I would have slipped into a drama role (and I frequently do!), it would have justified her illusion that I was mean and unfair and added fuel to the fire, diverting energy away from responsible behavior and towards drama. So many things I wanted to say, like "Hey, you know the rules, give it up!" (Persecutor), or "What part of 2000 don't you understand?" (Persecutor), or "I'm sorry, I'll make an exception this time. Just don't tell your mom." (Victim).

Because I want (instead of expect) my daughter to learn responsible use of her phone, I stay open to her struggle, resourceful with solutions, and persistent about the boundaries.

The same principles can be applied to workplace conversations. We routinely use this model to coach leaders on how to have difficult conversations with their peers, employees, and superiors. By wanting without expecting, leaders are able to be effective instead of justified.

Paul Unruh, a mentor of mine (Jeff) and man whom I respect as much as any person on the planet, once advised me, "If you take credit for your child's success then you must take credit for their failures." This is a powerful admonition about the impact of wants versus expectations. Wanting instead of expecting while staying in the Compassion Triangle allows a child, employee, or student to discover and internalize their motivators, maintain their dignity, and become who they are meant to be. Parenting from within the Compassion Triangle builds capable and competent young adults. If you'd like to learn more about parenting from the Compassion Triangle, we recommend reading *Building Self-Reliant Children in a Self-Indulgent World* by Glenn & Nelson.[1]

The beauty of the word *want* is that it helps bring focus to being responsible to others for our behavior because it clarifies where true motivation ultimately comes from. "I want to make 80 percent of my free throws" is a great statement of desire and implies a content

---

1 Glenn, S. and Nelson, J. (2000). *Raising Self-Reliant Children in a Self-Indulgent World: Seven Building Blocks For Raising Capable Young People*. Prima Publishing, Roseville, CA.

expectation (goal), yet it does not imply anyone else is responsible for making it happen. In addition, it naturally supports taking responsibility towards that goal while leaving open the possibility that there could be multiple ways to get there. For one player, it may mean shooting for an extra 15 minutes after practice each day. For another, it may mean putting on headphones and shooting free throws while jamming to his favorite music. For still another player, healthy competition with a teammate may work best. In each case, the content goal is to get better at free throws, while the unique motivational strategies are the process. And, in each case, the coach or parent can be extremely effective when staying in the Compassion Triangle with the player. Let's illustrate with a few examples:

> **Coach:** "You have been shooting 60 percent on your free throws. As often as you get fouled, increasing that to 80 percent could get us five additional points per game. I want you to increase your shooting percentage to at least 70 percent." (Open)
> **Player:** "I want to increase my percentage to 80 percent." (Open)
> **Coach:** "Terrific. Would you like any help on achieving that goal?" (Open and Resourceful)
> **Player:** "No thanks, Coach. I know what to do. May I stay after practice and work on free throws?" (Persistence)
> **Coach:** "Absolutely. I'll be here if you would like any pointers, and I will continue tracking your stats. I want starters to shoot at least 70 percent free throws." (Resourceful and Persistent)

In the Compassion Triangle, we can simultaneously be persistent with our goals and standards for behavior, open about our feelings and wants, and resourceful in how we help motivate ourselves and others towards those goals.

Let's see how this same interaction could have transpired in the Drama Triangle.

Coach: "You are a horrible free throw shooter! 60 percent is unacceptable. You should be scoring at least 5 more points per game. I expect you to improve." (Persecutor)

Player: "Sorry, Coach. I let the team down." (Victim)

Coach: "I don't need sorry. I need free throws." (Persecutor)

Player: "OK. I'll do better next time." (Victim)

Coach: "You better not let me and your team down or you'll be sitting on the bench!" (Persecutor)

OK, we know exactly what some of you are saying now. We really do! You might be saying, "I'm in a management position. I have to have expectations for my employees or they'll never get anything done. And, I've seen the research showing that clear expectations are one of the most important drivers of productivity and engagement."

We have two answers for you. First of all, you are 100 percent right, zero percent wrong. Expressing a want is not a get-out-of-jail-free card. Compassion is not a "hug a thug" program. This is hard work. Content expectations are necessary and very effective. People want to know what the goals are, what constitutes success, and where they stand. They want to know that you will hold them accountable in a supportive way. It is only when expectations cross the line and become process projections that things can get problematic between employees and supervisors.

One example of a process projection is overly rigid policies that prescribe how a job is to be done even when there might be many different, effective ways to do it. Or, consider a supervisor who micromanages an employee, frequently checking in while she works on a task, continually giving reminders about how it could or should be done, or offering methods and systems that could help without asking if the employee wants support. The impact is that employees feel micromanaged, stifled, and disrespected. Under these circumstances, employees will be less likely to come clean about their mistakes and ask for your support. They will secretly resist and their performance will ultimately suffer. They will complain about you to their coworkers and friends.

The second answer is that having a clear outcome goal is different from the process of how we achieve that goal. When supervisors confuse the goal with the methods, all sorts of unfortunate stuff can happen, including problems with morale, productivity, and engagement. Google has this figured out. Google has very aggressive and clearly articulated expectations for performance. And, everything from their work environment to their policies on how time is used, to the nature of supervision is open, resourceful, and persistent. They've allowed people to navigate their own path towards the goals while having clear content expectations. Their ability to know the difference between content and process, and leverage both, is a key to their success.

We regularly help our clients discipline and terminate employees from within the compassion triangle. Almost always, the result is behavior improvement and strengthened relationships or a dignified departure. Routinely, our clients have shared that employees who have been let go in this way later thanked them, saying it was the best thing that could have happened and they are a better person for it.

Expectations and Entitlement

The Millennial Generation has been accused of being entitled. They want raises and promotions and C-suite positions long before they have put in the time or earned the right. They jump ship if they aren't happy. They want transfers because they don't believe their skills are being put to good use. Ironically, as their predecessors, we are reaping what we sowed. These young adults were raised in the age of self-esteem, where everybody got a prize, no one was left out, and to be OK you just looked in the mirror and repeated the phrase, "I'm good enough, smart enough, and doggone it, people like me." Stuart Smalley from "Saturday Night Live" was the face of the self-esteem generation.

Research by Roy Baumeister and his colleagues at Florida State University has brought attention to the unintended consequences of nurturing self-esteem. High self-esteem is associated with narcissism, inability to accept constructive criticism, low tolerance for frustration and failure, and an attitude of entitlement.

Before we Baby Boomers get too self-righteous, let me suggest that we tend to feel quite entitled as well. We believe that just because we expect someone to do something, they will. We assume that expectations are sufficient, and that by stating them with enough authority, from a position of power or experience, people will act accordingly. To take it one step further, we have convinced ourselves that the time and energy we've put in to achieve our position will somehow motivate and inspire others to work hard for us. We lead by example!

Higher education is one of the most entitled places on the planet. When I've approached professors with the question of who's responsible for the learning that takes place in the classroom, there are usually two camps. One camp, which I call the Educator Camp, see their mission to engage students, inspire learning, find ways to make the material come alive for their students. They want, without expecting, their students to learn. Consequently, they share responsibility for motivating students in diverse ways. These professors don't always publish the most articles, but they are the ones students remember — the ones who made a difference in their lives. Their learning standards (content expectations) are just as high as anyone else.

The second camp, which I call the Entitled Camp, are the pure academics. They believe that it is the students' responsibility to learn from them. Grudgingly, they take time out of their valuable research schedules to lecture a class. Their duty, say these professors, is to be smart, achieve tenure and publish. The students' job is to figure out what the heck they are talking about. The Entitled Camp is arrogant, self-righteous, and out of touch.

Variations on these two camps exist in all sectors and professions. Camp one who expects others to do what they say from an entitled position. Camp two who wants others to be successful and share responsibility for the process of how that gets done in a spirit of humility.

"In time of change, learners inherit the earth while the learned find themselves beautifully equipped to deal with a world that no longer exists."

- Eric Hoffer

We propose that the left-brained, linear, industrial, mechanical approach to leadership is more prone to entitlement. Persons within these cultures have often worked very hard to move up through the ranks. Many have invested in specific education for their jobs, have learned to delay gratification, and are accustomed to a culture that values experience, hard work, and longevity. Each of these characteristics can lead to attitudes of superiority and entitlement. Entitlement in this context does not mean that I expect to have things without working for them. It means that I expect others to be motivated like me, to do it the way I did it, to earn it fair and square, to "pull themselves up by their bootstraps." In its own way, this attitude is just as self-centered and limiting as what we criticize in the up-and-coming generation. This approach to performance and motivation is increasingly insufficient for the Process Age.

Expectations, Guilt, and Shame

Expectations can be another slippery slope. Fair warning: This one may get a little more uncomfortable for readers, and may stir up baggage from past relationships. We're going to be talking about guilt and shame.

Like us, many of you probably grew up in families where your parents used guilt with extreme precision and impact. Do any of these phrases ring a bell; "Shame on you!," "You should have known better," "First, you have to admit you were wrong," or "I expected more from you." How do you remember feeling at that moment? Afraid? Embarrassed? Ashamed? I (Nate) felt all three. Did it inspire you to chart a new course for your life and find your true motivators? Not for me. At best, I dutifully complied, said what I was supposed to say, and secretly fantasized about revenge. At worst, I argued, made excuses, and joined my parents in the Drama Triangle. Amazingly, I see this dynamic at work as frequently today as I did as a child. My landscape has changed from parents to supervisors to spouse to colleagues, yet I continue to observe the negative power of process expectations in creating negative outcomes.

Guilt is a powerful motivator. It lets us know we've crossed a line, violated a boundary, or gone against our own standards of conduct. Guilt that comes from a healthy place within us can play a valuable guiding role in our lives. When I connect the dots between what I've done and what I know is right, the feeling I experience can engender the desire to take ownership of what to do next. As parents, supervisors, and leaders, we have a great opportunity to clarify our desired behaviors, standards, and content expectations. We can play a key role in holding up a mirror about behavior and performance. And, we can attempt to help people connect the dots for themselves.

Let's illustrate by returning to the first interaction between coach and player earlier in this chapter. The coach held up a mirror to his player, describing clearly the unwanted behavior and the desired alternative. He described the discrepancy respectfully, without questioning the integrity or dignity of the player. Even when the player expressed a desire for improved performance, the coach offered support without imposing a particular approach. And, while leaving it up to the player to find his own path towards better performance, the coach never let go of the content expectations of 70 percent free throw shooting. Furthermore, the coach was clear about consequences – the player could not start without a 70 percent free throw average. If he was unable to meet those expectations, the choice and responsibility would have still been his. He could ask for help, try something different, or deal with the consequences.

We claim that we want people to own their behavior, admit they made a mistake, and say they are sorry. But when it's not delivered to our satisfaction as teachers, parents, coaches, or supervisors, it is seductively easy to become personally invested in the person feeling guilty according to our criteria. We've all done it. If you've ever said to another person, "You have to admit you did it," or pressured someone to apologize for something, you have pushed guilt.

Pushing guilt violates a person's dignity in two ways. The first violation is trying to impose your motivation onto someone else. You know in your heart that if you had done that very same thing you'd feel guilty, and that guilt would motivate you to own up and make it right. Therefore, your logic says that the same should be true for the other person. Probably, at some point, you've successfully pressured someone to apologize. I bet you were disappointed that they didn't seem to mean it. One of my (Nate) father's favorite stories from his childhood includes the following scenario. As a young boy, hiding behind his mother's dress while she visited with an adult parishioner at a church function, he whispered loudly to her, "That lady looks like a horse," referring to the woman with whom his mother is conversing. His mother, mortified at her son's terrible manners, says to him, "Son, apologize to this nice lady for your rude comment." He looked the lady in the eye and said politely, "I am sorry you look like a horse."

The second violation when pushing guilt is that it relies on the myths of "I can make you feel bad emotionally" and "You can make me feel bad emotionally." Once we jump onto the Drama Triangle in a persecuting role and begin pushing guilt, we are sending messages to the other person that they not OK because they are not feeling, thinking, or acting the way we want them to. We rely on them buying into the victim myth and playing along. This is a win-lose scenario because when we fall into the persecutor role, there is no option for dignity or compassion. Guilt pushers seek primarily to feel justified, even when they are ineffective at influencing behavior in a positive way.

The use of guilt isn't just reserved for blatant Persecutors. Others use it effectively in more subtle ways. If you've ever heard someone say, "You're going to be the death of me," you've experienced passive-aggressive guilt. Instead of pushing guilt in an attacking way, the passive-aggressive approach attempts to get others to believe that they are responsible for another person's suffering and buy into the myth that "I can make you feel bad emotionally." Everyday parents, bosses, coaches, or spouses export their own embarrassment, feelings of inadequacy, or frustration onto others with statements such as "I don't know how much longer I can tolerate the comments people are making about you," or "You know how that makes me feel when you do that," or "You drove me to drink."

Pushing guilt onto someone is an empty victory, and in the broad scheme of things, it is ineffective. At best, it leads to compliance. At worst, it fosters a lifetime of self-doubt, internalized negative associations, and difficulty handling failure in a positive way. Some persons respond to guilt by avoiding responsibility at all costs so as to never have to experience it. Others find that the guilt takes on a life of its own, turns into shame, and leads to depression, self-damaging behavior, and a tendency to continually punish themselves. Still others project these negative feelings outward, repeating the cycle of guilt with the ones they love most by self-righteously attacking and instilling fear.

When guilt is pushed onto another person, he or she might experience shame. While guilt is about behavior, shame is about self-worth. Table 1 outlines the key differences between the two.

Behind the feeling of shame is the belief that "I am not OK," and an acceptance of the victim role on the Drama Triangle. Attempting to shame another person (i.e. push guilt and project our own motivators onto them) reflects the belief that "You are not OK" and assumes the persecutor role on the Drama Triangle. Everyday, these two do the drama dance in our families, communities, and organizations.

Guilt says..	Shame says..
"I did something wrong."	"I am wrong."
"I messed up."	"I am a screw-up."
"That's not OK."	"You are not OK."
"You crossed a boundary."	"You should be ashamed of yourself."

Table 1: Guilt vs. Shame

The tragic truth is that many organizations and families function for years, even decades, in the Drama Triangle. Persecutors find themselves in leadership positions and rule with fear and guilt while Victims find themselves in support positions, accepting that they are not OK and trying to perfectly please their bosses. The system sustains itself because everybody plays the game. The consequences: high turnover, chronic health problems, low morale, dissatisfied customers, and lost opportunity.

Following is a summary of the key concepts covered in this chapter. Accompanying each concept is a "So what?" and a "Now what?" to help you bring it all together and take effective action in your own life.

Concept	So what?	Now what?
Want	It's OK to want someone to learn and grow without expecting them to. Ultimately, I cannot control anybody but myself.	Be clear that your wants for someone else are yours, not necessarily theirs. Ask yourself if you are seeking to be effective (Compassion), or to feel justified (Drama). It's OK to have standards and enforce those standards compassionately.
Expect	Content expectations can be productive. Process expectations cause power struggles because we project our motivational needs onto others.	Focus on specific behaviors and goals. Develop skills to recognize and appreciate different motivational needs. Assist others to pursue goals using their own motivational needs.
Entitlement	The biggest threat to future success is past success. What worked for you may not work for others.	Don't expect that your experience or example is sufficient to inspire and motivate others. Move beyond yourself and into the lives of those you lead.
Guilt	Guilt can be healthy when it motivates an intrinsic desire to improve.	Stop insisting that people feel guilty. Start focusing on specific behaviors that will make things right.

Concept	So what?	Now what?
Shame	Guilt can turn to shame when either of these myths are believed and acted on: "I can make you feel bad emotionally," or "You can make me feel bad emotionally."	Focus on the behavior and content expectations rather than on the person. Be Open, Resourceful, and Persistent

Table 2: Summary of Expectations-related Concepts with Implications and Action Steps

Leading from the Compassion Triangle

The number one predictor of job satisfaction is an employee's relationship with her immediate supervisor. It is well known that people leave leaders, not jobs. So what makes for a strong and engaging supervisory relationship? We've reviewed the literature on engagement and productivity, drawn from our experience in all types of business settings, and read hundreds of white papers, online discussions, and blogs on this topic.

The current best practices in leadership appear to conform very closely with what we outlined in the table above. The best leaders are those who:

- are aware of their own agendas, motivators, and emotional make-up
- are clear about what they want without expecting others to be motivated the same way
- understand the complex nature of diversity and how to leverage it toward shared goals

- are able to distinguish a person's behavior from the person
- articulate clear goals and give helpful feedback
- avoid shaming others
- have the humility to choose effectiveness instead of self-justification

In short, the best leaders lead from within the Compassion Triangle. Inspired individuals and companies have built cultures from within the Compassion Triangle.

So far in this book, we have outlined the distinction between process and content. We've introduced the Drama Triangle as a framework to understand unhealthy relationship dynamics. Next, we envisioned what the healthy alternative can look like through the lens of the Compassion Triangle. Then, we got specific by describing the dynamics of distress along with tools to assess yourself and your team. Beginning with Chapter 8, "May I Have Your Attention?" we began charting the course for change through an understanding of positive influence and psychological motivators, as well as the predictable ways that humans wield negative influence in the Drama Triangle. In this chapter, we've explored how expectations can pull people into Drama, and we have offered some positive alternatives.

Next, we move on to the dynamics of change. Assuming you'd like to spend less time in drama and more time in compassion, how can you achieve that goal? How do people change and what tools will help you navigate that journey?

CHAPTER 11

Change and Drama

"Life is change. Growth is optional. Choose wisely."

— Karen Kaiser Clark

Moving from Drama to Compassion is a constant and daily process. In this chapter we will describe the nature of the change challenges we are facing in the Process Age. We will argue that more than ever, change is a process, not an event, and therefore requires process tools to navigate. In the next two chapters, we will outline a model of change that will help you negotiate this new landscape and provide guidelines on navigating change with compassion instead of drama. Ultimately, our goal is to provide resources for you to recognize and take advantage of key choice points in your life where you can be intentional about growing in a positive direction.

First, let's take a look at the nature of change in the Process Age.

Change is Constant

There's lots of talk about how change is happening faster and faster every day and how information is doubling at an ever-increasing rate. There was a time when a single library in Europe held all the books that had been written. Essentially all knowledge was held in this library. And, there were people who had read all the books in the library. So, one could infer that there were people who knew everything there was to know! Today, we don't just use search engines, we use decision engines to help us navigate the mushrooming body of information in the world. A TV ad several years ago showed a man on his computer searching the Internet. At one point he stops, sits up, and exclaims, "I have reached the end of the Internet!" The irony of this situation is that within days, hours or perhaps minutes, the body of knowledge available to this man has doubled.

To use a computer metaphor, consider the concept of upgrading. Upgrading implies that your old technology, whether it's your hard drive, operating system, or monitor, no longer serves your needs well. Your computer has become inefficient, slow, unreliable, unable to deal with new software. In short, it's a dinosaur. To upgrade means to replace portions of the computer in order to re-establish effective functioning.

Upgrading used to be an event, a discrete point in time where a specific action was taken that had significant, noticeable impact. That impact lasted for a decent length of time during which you didn't need to worry about it. Fifteen years ago you could upgrade a computer every couple of years. Add a little more memory, replace the hard drive, and you were good to go.

In terms of broader human change, upgrading used to be an event as well. Values, perspectives, and traditions were upgraded perhaps once in a generation. Parents upgraded child raising methods from the model their parents used. We upgraded our 20-year-old washer and dryer to new models that were more efficient. Then we were good to go for another 10–20 years.

Fast forward to the present. We live in an age of perpetual beta. Rather than going through extensive testing and perfecting, many products are released rapidly, allowing the consumer to be part of the development phase. The software on your computer is updated every time you go online. Your phone's operating system can be upgraded whenever necessary without your even knowing it. Your calendar and contact list can be synched automatically. Your apps are receiving updates whenever you are online. Even the maps in your car navigation system can be updated in real time as road conditions change.

The rapid increase in available information has led to provocative questions: What's the difference between information and knowledge? What new skills are required to make sense of it all? Where does wisdom fit in? What might be the unintended consequences of this ongoing information explosion? What we do know is that we are facing change at an ever-increasing pace, and our old ways of coping are becoming less effective.

Change is Insidious

Because we are virtually connected all the time, change is happening for us and to us without our knowledge or deliberate involvement. Through every little choice we make, whether it's the decision to sync our calendars every 15 minutes, or to allow software updates to happen automatically, we are becoming less and less aware and intentional about the changes that affect our lives. Eventually, we may wonder who's in charge — are we, or the technology?

My wife and I (Nate) have two teenage daughters who have cell phones. Recently I went downstairs to my oldest daughter's bedroom to tell her goodnight and conduct our usual routine of reflecting on the day, anticipating what's coming up tomorrow, and wishing her a good night. I was taken aback when I walked into her room and she was texting with a friend. Ignoring me completely, she continued to text as I tried to get her attention. Finally, I raised my voice enough to bother her, and she said impatiently, "Dad, wait a minute, I am trying to finish this conversation with my friend."

I left her room, angry and frustrated. As I tried to explain my reaction to my wife, I found myself wondering out loud, "How did this happen?" When did our daughter become so disrespectful and disengaged from us? How has she lost sight of what's important? She's addicted to that damn phone!" As I processed my feelings I began to realize that my daughter's attachment to her phone didn't just "happen." What I experienced was not an event. It was the insidious nature of change. We arrived at this moment because of many little choices along the way that culminated in an event-like wake-up call, something that was so emotionally significant that I couldn't ignore or tolerate it. I began to look back and take stock. We bought our daughter the phone. We decided to add her to our unlimited everything plan. We upgraded her to a smartphone. We set up the conditions for this to happen.

We blame the phone as well. It's sexy, easy to use, rewards her with beeps, buzzes, vibrations, and notices, and allows her to feel connected to all her friends all the time. How can a parent possibly compete with this seductive instrument?

I can't decide which role in the Drama Triangle I want to play. I could dive into the persecutor role and blame some sneaky, fiendish plot by Apple or Sprint or Google to addict children and divide families though their products. I could attack my daughter for her behavior and take her phone away. Or, I could slip on the rescuer mantle and overfunction for my daughter by trying to manage her phone use, so I could avoid my feelings of despair. Alternatively, I could play victim and simply resign myself to the reality. I just want it all to go away. But I can't. We are too far in to go back.

The solution unfolds each day in my household. When I stay open I can be receptive to the needs, wants, and feelings of my children. Resourcefulness helps us all find win-win solutions. Persistence keeps us on track with what's most important, upholding promises and enforcing boundaries that we've agreed to.

Many great writers have explored this phenomenon of the unintended consequences of our technological age. If you are interested in further reading on the topic, we recommend starting with the work of Marshall McLuhan or Shane Hipps.

A Challenge to Institutions

In our work with corporations, churches, and schools, we repeatedly experience this dynamic: Companies everywhere are struggling to know what to do about social media. Do we ban it during work? Do we attempt to leverage it for the greater good? How can we control something that is so insidious and omnipresent? The advantages are promoted as obvious and overwhelming, and we are encouraged by the masses to "go with the flow, get onboard, and up with the times!" Yet somewhere down deep, we know it's not all good.

Faith communities struggle with the changing face of congregational life, the changing needs and wants of communities, and the impact of technology and mobility on how people participate. Do you want to attend an Internet-based virtual congregation? How about scan a QR (Quick Response) code on the church bulletin and get instant access to the church's website. Don't carry cash; just swipe your credit card from your pew.

Do we embrace change and adapt wholeheartedly to reach more people? If so, what are the consequences of this to our message and core mission? What must change and what cannot change in order for us to maintain our identity? Who are we and who are we becoming? It's easy to argue that change has always been part of church life and that previous generations have engaged in the same struggle. But it is unequivocally not the same. Constant and insidious change are new dynamics that previous generations did not face to the same degree. The Process Age brings with it new and different change challenges.

Schools are perhaps hit the hardest and struggle the most to cope with constant and insidious change. If knowledge is expanding and changing so quickly, then what is the mission and role of education? The content of most texbooks are at least a decade behind what's happening on the cutting edge. What children learn will be obsolete in a few years. If our duty in education is to prepare students for the world ahead, what does that mean? Does it mean making sure they are competent in all the latest technology? If so, the resource burden on schools is nearly unbearable. Does it mean making sure they are equipped with process tools for navigating a rapidly changing world? If so, this challenges the very foundation of our education system which was built on an industrial, linear, logical, left-brained, content-based paradigm.

Change Models for the Process Age

Don't lose hope. There are change models for the Process Age. We've chosen one we believe offers excellent perspective and tools for navigating our lives in the Process Age. We aren't claiming this is the best or only model, but it's one that we have found very helpful. We encourage you to explore several different change theories to see what helps you move forward. Good models can help individuals, teams, companies, and communities embark on a healthy journey of change from within the Compassion Triangle.

Beck's Change Model

Don Beck is a leading global authority on value systems and societal change. He has worked behind the scenes in very high-profile system change settings, including Nelson Mandela's transition to leader of a black democracy in South Africa and peace negotiations in the Middle East. Elaborating and extending the work on biopsychosocial systems originated by the late Clare W. Graves, Beck has developed Spiral Dynamics Integral, a model of systems and value change.[1] We have found this model to be both simple and useful in a wide range of applications. While a complete overview of this model is beyond the scope of this chapter, we will summarize his framework for how change happens, adding our interpretations and implications.

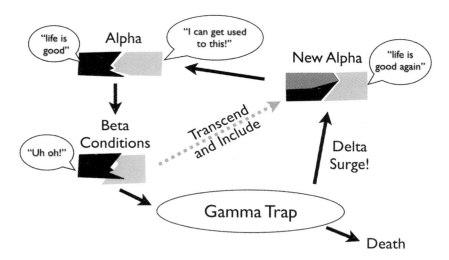

Figure 1. Beck's model of change consists of four stages that flow in a cycle to describe the evolving process of change.

Alpha Conditions

Alpha Conditions are present when the way we do things is a good fit with life conditions. Our standard coping mechanisms, habits, traditions,

1 Beck, D. and Cowan, C. (2003). *Spiral Dynamics: Mastering Values, Leadership and Change*. Blackwell Publishing, Malden, MA.

values, and approaches get the job done with minimal discomfort. It could be as simple as the fact that my five-year-old washing machine adequately cleans five loads per week and gives me no trouble. Or, it could be more complex, such as a church's values, processes, and systems effectively supporting their community outreach mission. In enterprise, it may relate to the systems and structures that support the strategic plan and current business model.

Alpha conditions are characterized by minimal effort and intention since habits have been established, routines are automatic, and inertia keeps things going. Life is good.

Beta Conditions

Unfortunately, while our habits, routines, and processes generally do not change without conscious effort, life conditions do. Regardless of our wishes, life changes constantly and insidiously. Beta Conditions arise when life conditions change significantly enough to cause tension and discomfort. "Uh oh!" is the simplest expression to describe the experience of Beta Conditions. We wake up one day and wonder what happened. We realize that we are having an increasingly difficult time accomplishing the same goals with existing methods. We are working harder for the same results. There seem to be glitches in the system. Our metrics are showing concerning trends.

Beta conditions leave us with at least two key choices, one drama-based the other compassion-based. We'll follow the drama path in this chapter, and outline the compassionate alternative in the chapter that follows.

The Gamma Trap

Beta conditions can easily precipitate drama responses, all of which lead to dead ends. The Gamma Trap is the dead end street of doing more of the same while expecting different results.

Victim reactions include comments such as:

"We're screwed!"
"What happened?"
"Why didn't anybody tell me?"
"It's all our fault; we should have seen it coming."
"Who moved my cheese?"
"We'll never make it through."
"This is a sign of something terrible."

Each of these responses reflects passivity, lack of confidence, a distorted sense of control, and unhealthy vulnerability.

Persecutor reactions to Beta Conditions include aggressive, blaming statements such as:

"You were supposed to let us know."
"You were in charge of forecasting and missed the indicators."
"If everybody didn't have their heads in the sand, we'd be fine."
"Our traditions served us just fine, they are good enough for the next generation as well."
"Our old plan will work if you people just work harder and are more committed."

Behind the Persecutor's responses is the attitude that someone else's lack of competence, intelligence or commitment is to blame for problems. These responses also reflect a lack of responsibility and delusional thinking by assuming that someone or something could have prevented the Beta Conditions — that controlling life conditions is even possible.

Rescuer reactions to Beta Conditions reflect haphazard attempts to fix, console, make peace, put out fires, downplay, or otherwise avoid the real issues.

> *"It's not as bad as everybody says, don't worry."*
> *"I'll come in on the weekend to help get us through this."*
> *"Here are some great books on change you should read."*
> *"Let's bring in someone to do a lunch n' learn."*

Rescuers try to do or think for others, and then feel like martyrs because they've sacrificed time and energy without getting the recognition they crave.

In the Gamma trap, drama is the norm. Companies react haphazardly instead of responding with intention and balance. Organizations seek to be justified instead of effective. Individuals deny that anything is wrong while they turn up the volume on the routines that may have worked during alpha conditions but are no longer effective. They cling to false or outdated assumptions, stuck in behavior that Albert Einstein called insanity, trying the same thing over and over and expecting different results.

A real case study will illustrate. A healthcare institution was experiencing increasing turnover. Times were changing with old-timers retiring, a younger workforce coming in, payer mixes changing, and consumers seeking different types of services. Traditionally, this organization had relied on staff loyalty, long tenure, and a private "we are family" environment that kept much information hidden and also kept employees compliant through fear and guilt. They rested on their laurels of tradition, excellence, and dominance in their particular market niche.

It was brought to the attention of leaders in this organization that practitioners were leaving to seek greener pastures, sometimes shortly after receiving valuable training. The leaders' reaction: require a strict payback contract before an employee could receive special training. This policy, they thought, would reinforce commitment, loyalty, and reduce money wasted on people who would only take their new skills to another organization. At the very least, it would protect their investment.

The result was that employees began to either skip the training, pay out of pocket for the training instead of signing a payback clause, or simply leave the organization altogether. The leaders' drama reaction was to intensify their habitual ways of coping (fear, secrecy, and loyalty) instead of recognizing that changing life conditions required new ways of coping. What this organization failed to recognize was that a different, younger workforce sought flexibility, freedom, opportunities for advancement, and respect.

When leaders are stuck in the gamma trap, they refuse to change anything about their values, systems, and processes in the face of new life conditions. What does change, however, is the level of discomfort experienced by everyone involved and the pileup of negative consequences.

Once entrenched in the Gamma trap, there is no going back, says Beck. There is usually a point of no return where a painless transition is no longer realistic or possible. The rut is too deep. Life conditions are so out of sync with entrenched habits that graceful adaptation is impossible.

All is not lost. While there is no going back, there are new, different outcomes and choices available. The upside is that change is still possible. The downside is that once into Gamma Trap, change is extremely painful and always includes collateral damage. Let's look at two choices still available to persons and organizations in the Gamma trap.

Death and Renewal

One way out of the Gamma trap is the death of the organization. Some are slow deaths, such as churches that get smaller and smaller until there aren't enough people to pay the bills. Some are more dramatic, such as takeovers, dissolutions or bankruptcies. Sometimes the fragments of organizations move on, rebuild, attempt to heal, regroup, and start over. The common theme is that life as we know it is over. This pattern has been repeating for thousands of years in nature as well as within our human institutions.

Revolution

Revolution is another way out of the Gamma trap and involves upheaval, tearing down the old to build the new. Revolution is not a house renovation. It is a demolition. Revolution can involve people rising up and taking over, such as when governments are toppled by angry citizens. Or it can involve an outside entity forcefully taking control of a sinking ship. In organizations this may take the form of a parent company sending in an outside leader to clean house and install a new business model. Either way, suffering has become so great that the only alternative to death is to dismantle and begin again. Sometimes the end result bears little resemblance to its predecessor.

Revolution involves carnage and collateral damage. People get hurt, communities and families are shaken, and there are usually long-term consequences. While it's not what we would want for ourselves, sometimes this is how it happens. Again, this is no different than the cycles in our natural world.

Fortunately, revolution isn't the only way forward. Remember those pesky Beta conditions? Remember that there was also a compassionate option? Let's turn to it now.

CHAPTER 12

Change and Compassion: Transcend and Include

When we find ourselves in beta conditions, the gamma trap is neither inevitable nor the only option. There is a healthier alternative, an evolutionary process called Transcend and Include.

Transcend means to surpass or go beyond limits. Usually, this word is used to describe a movement to a higher-order state of being, a rising above process in which drama and negativity are left behind in favor of a more enlightened approach. Transcend is different from other change words. For example, it does not mean to replace, as this would be like throwing the baby out with the bath water. It is not the same as transition, as this implies moving from one thing to the next without clarifying "from what to what." Transcending is a process of evolution from what worked once upon a time to modes that work better now. Transcending is absent of ego and self-justification and instead seeks effectiveness. Transcend also refers to overarching principles or values that defy time and space. We often speak of good design, good art, or good philosophy as transcending time and context. Good design, for example, endures because of its process, not the content.

How do I transcend the pull of a smart phone? By focusing on its relationship to those things that defy time and space; relationships, connection, communication, values, and one's sense of self within the world. These process themes are always relevant, regardless of the content we're dealing with. Transcending means evolving our *how* so that we can again do the *what* of our lives more effectively.

Inclusion is also a critical part of evolving change. History, tradition, wisdom, and experience are vital to our future. If those who do not learn from history are destined to repeat it, then it is paramount to retain and include what is useful, what has been learned, and what can provide clues for a successful future. This very often involves process themes more than content, strategy more than task. For example, Henry Ford's famous quote, "The biggest threat to future success is past success," is a process idiom that transcends industry or time.

A learning organization is the term given to an enterprise that facilitates the learning of its members and continuously transforms itself.[1] For those seeking to learn more about evolving organizational change and avoiding gamma traps, we highly recommend the work of Peter Senge.[2]

Learning organizations have developed cultural processes to support a transcend and include approach to changing life conditions. This approach to change recognizes that change is constant and insidious, and does not wait for gamma traps to make necessary adjustments.

The following features characterize a transcend and include approach to change.

- respects history without being confined by it
- nimble without being fickle
- committed without being entrenched

1 Pedler, M., Burgogyne, J. and Boydell, T. (1997). *The Learning Company: A Strategy for Sustainable Development*. 2nd Ed. London; McGraw-Hill
2 Senge, P. (1990). The Fifth Discipline: The Art and Practice of the Learning Organization. Doubleday/Currency.

- open, resourceful, and persistent

We believe that individuals and organizations can only transcend and include from within the compassion triangle.

As we've discussed, the purpose of conflict is to create. Conflict represents the potential for something new to be brought into the world, something that will transcend and include what has been before. Much like the grain of sand that is transformed into a pearl by the oyster, the discomfort of conflict has the potential for creative new life.

But conflict has the potential to create only when dealt with during beta conditions and from within the compassion triangle. Waiting or avoiding until you are in the clutches of the gamma trap ensures conditions for destructive conflict.

Beta conditions represent conflict between what is, what has been, and what is yet to come. The gamma trap represents a drama-based reaction to conflict, one that destroys. To transcend and include is a compassion-based response to conflict that encourages creativity and sets the stage for what's next.

Table 1 summarizes the many attitudes and approaches we can take during times of change. In addition to the new themes introduced in this chapter, we have repeated earlier concepts to illustrate how well compassion triangle dynamics support healthy change.

Gamma Trap - DRAMA	Evolve Change - COMPASSION
More of the same	Transcend
Throw baby out with the bath water	Include what has served us well
Reactive and defensive	Proactive and discerning
Rigid	Nimble
Defined by the past	Learn from the past
Fear, secrecy, and guilt	Anticipation, transparency, and engagement
Change as threat	Change as opportunity
Conflict that destroys	Conflict that creates
Tunnel vision	Perspective
Delusional; believes things can be like they used to be	In touch with reality; sees change as a natural part of life
Failing backward	Failing forward
Excessive collateral damage	Limited collateral damage
Leads to revolution or death	Leads to higher forms of effectiveness

Table 1. A summary of Drama and Compassion-based responses to Beta Conditions

Delta Surge and the New Alpha

While there is less collateral damage with evolution than with revolution, both lead to what Beck has coined the "Delta Surge." A rush of new energy and excitement arises from having more effective ways of meeting life's demands, originating in the development of new value systems and perspectives. Discomfort is greatly reduced. People are talking to one another again, optimism is in the air, and growth is stabilizing. It becomes easier to appreciate the pain and effort that got us here because we are experiencing new benefits each day. Those who have remained, along with any new blood, have discovered the thrill of a new course, new vistas, and new opportunities. In effect, delta surge is the payoff for our effort and suffering. It is the awakening of what's next. Even out of the greatest pain comes new growth and potential.

The delta surge paves the way for the New Alpha. When new life conditions are met with new ways of coping, life feels good again. There is a fit, and balance is restored to the system.

Alas, because change is constant and insidious, even the new alpha soon becomes just plain old alpha, and the cycle repeats. Since the greatest threat to future success is past success, getting too comfortable in the new alpha only results in a rude awakening in the face of the next beta conditions.

Dealing well with change isn't something we do automatically. Nor does it become easier because we've been through it before. Changing gracefully and effectively requires skills and tools. Becoming adept at using these tools will make change easier to handle. And, because change is a process, not an event, process solutions are required.

Applying Beck's Cycle to Leadership

Below is a simple checklist to help you diagnose where you, your team, and your organization currently are on Beck's cycle of change. Check any statements that apply to your context. Use it individually or with your team to guide conversation about next steps.

Alpha Conditions

____ The way we are doing things works well with minimal adjustment.

____ Our routines and procedures are effective at supporting our goals.

____ Our values and philosophy support our progress.

Next Steps: Stay aware, keep doing what you are doing, but don't get complacent. Periodically try new things just for the heck of it. Keep your eye on the future. Watch your metrics for leading indicators.

Leadership Responsibilities and Opportunities: Encourage new employees who ask "why." Embrace the re-asking of old questions. Support a culture of failing forward. Don't allow veteran employees to get by without challenging themselves and learning something new every day. Focus on refining existing processes and procedures. Get at least some of your education outside your field, whether it involves what you read, conferences you attend, or mentors with whom you affiliate.

Beta Conditions

____ Things aren't the same as they used to be.

____ We're expending more energy for the same results.

____ The way we are doing things doesn't seem to be working as well as it once did.

Next Steps: Evaluate, get an outside perspective, ask others what they are seeing and doing. Question outdated assumptions and habits. Take some new risks. Remember, there are no stupid questions. Invest proactively in skills to help you and your team become more open, resourceful, and persistent. Communication training and teambuilding are excellent at this time because they create a safer space for new perspectives to come forth and help people break out of ineffective habits.

Leadership Responsibilities and Opportunities: Stay open! Hunkering down is the surest way into the gamma trap. Encourage and be a role model for curiosity, enthusiasm, and optimism. Look to the fringes of your organization and profession for new ideas; many concepts that we fully accept today were once seen as crazy ideas by the status quo. Resist the urge to focus too heavily on cost-cutting at the expense of innovation. While everyone else is hunkering down, you should be anticipating and designing the next big thing! We are not discouraging a careful look at how money is being spent, as long as the focus is on challenging outdated assumptions and processes. Shotgun approaches that seek to cut costs anywhere possible often result in reduced morale, fear and uncertainty, and failure to see and confront elephants in the room.

During beta conditions, invest in training and leadership development, specifically in new and upcoming technical job skills you've identified, as well as in process skills of communication, leadership, and innovation. A friend of mine who works for a national investment firm shared how the company uses periods of economic downturn and uncertainty to train employees. Instead of seeing smaller workloads as threats, they see it as an opportunity to help their employees grow and excel. The rationale is that when things turn around and new opportunities manifest, everyone else is playing catch-up while their employees are trained and ready to seize opportunity. It works for them.

We started Next Element in October 2008, the month that the global recession was officially declared by financial experts. Without exception, all the companies who hired us and took the time and resources to invest in quality leadership development and communication skills training are still in business today, doing well and growing. They weathered the storms like we all did. And, they found ways to transcend and include. We don't share this story to boast about our services, rather to show evidence of the benefits of investing in your people during beta conditions.

Gamma Trap (DRAMA)

____ We feel doomed and at the mercy of outside forces.
____ We are fighting with ourselves and others about what to do.
____ We are trying more of the same, hoping things will turn around.
____ We convince ourselves that anyone who is not suffering like we are is just lucky or getting an unfair break.

Next Steps: Get outside help immediately! Develop skills for being Open, Resourceful and Persistent. Communication and conflict-resolution training, team building, and serious examination of your structure and processes are paramount at this time. Although dramatic content solutions may seem appealing, they are unlikely to succeed because drama perpetuates drama. Drama-based cultures will eat content solutions for lunch!

Break the cycle of drama in your organization. Get rid of people who you've known for years have been toxic to your organization but somehow maintain positions of power. Promote and support people who are willing to take innovative risks and stay out of drama. Find your natural leaders at any level and give them wings. Seek, support, and promote diversity because it is your key to innovation and evolution.

Leadership Responsibilities and Opportunities: If you can't or won't change yourself and your approach to leadership immediately, do everyone a favor and get out. Stop making excuses for yourself or anyone else. Stop tolerating drama within your own team or among those you lead. It's better to make a bad personnel decision than make no decision at all. If your preaching and threats are covering up your own fear that you can't save everyone, get help and get honest with yourself and others. If you are bottling up your anger thinking that you can absorb everyone else's suffering, get help and get honest. If you are trying to control everything and everyone to avoid the reality that you are losing control, get help and get honest. If you are putting off taking care of yourself believing that you'll get to that later, get help and get honest.

Evolving Change (COMPASSION)

    ___ We are confident in our ability to fail forward.
    ___ We are creative and flexible.
    ___ We are transparent with each other and aware of the conditions around us.

Next Steps: Continually sharpen your process skills of openness, resourcefulness and persistence. Evolving change requires extreme courage. Support each other and stay connected. Celebrate even the smallest successes. Tend to your wounds and don't ignore the pain involved.

Leadership Responsibilities and Opportunities: "Let no pain go unused." I don't know how many times I (Nate) heard this from a mentor of mine. It definitely made an impression on me, and I think it's a terrific guiding principle for leadership. A leader's ability to anticipate, support, and learn positive lessons from pain is a key to being ready for the next beta conditions. New alpha conditions can quickly turn toxic if care isn't taken to ensure that old memories, old wounds, and old cultural permissions have been resolved. Leaders must create and support new cultures and habits, and quickly nip in the bud any hints of "us vs. them" or "the good old days." Looking forward is the key. Respecting the past is OK only if it focuses on positive learnings and reinforces compassion-based approaches going forward.

In this chapter we've addressed how change is dealt with in both the drama and compassion triangles. We've outlined a model of change that can help put things in perspective, and offered tools to diagnose and treat the stress of change you are experiencing. Next, we will explore the topic of intention and the power of the self-fulfilling prophecy.

CHAPTER 13

From Attention to Intention

"Man often becomes what he believes himself to be. If I keep on saying to myself that I cannot do a certain thing, it is possible that I may end by really becoming incapable of doing it. On the contrary, if I have the belief that I can do it, I shall surely acquire the capacity to do it even if I may not have it at the beginning."

—Mahatma Gandhi

"Whether you think you can or you think you can't, you are right."

—Henry Ford

In their book, *Switch*,[1] Chip and Dan Heath tell of a story of British Petroleum (BP), one of the world's most successful drilling companies, notwithstanding the recent catastrophe in the Gulf. For BP, success was defined as hitting oil on one out of every five wells. They we very aware that four out of five times they did not achieve success. They focused their attention on a 20 percent success rate. BP also knew that when their explorers, those who searched out places to drill, predicted that a well had a 75 percent chance of success, the actual success rate was nearly 100 percent.

BP decided to change its strategy from one out of five to "No Dry Holes." This redefined success as five out of five, not one out of five. The drillers focused only on wells that had a 75 percent chance of success. This shift catapulted BP to obscene profitability. The No Dry Holes strategy dramatically shifted the company's return on investment.

If you could move from one out of five to five out of five, would you? And what would it take for you to make that leap? It's not as obvious as it may seem. BP was not in the gamma trap. They may not even have been deep into beta conditions at the time of their shift to No Dry Holes. What they were able to do, however, is move from attention to intention. They transcended and included. They included the accumulated knowledge of welldrilling. It took no new knowledge to do what they did. At the same time, they transcended the *status quo* by questioning the accepted standards of success, and moved beyond an attentional, less focused approach to success. The result was a delta surge of mammoth proportions.

Webster defines attention as "the act, or state of applying the mind to something" and intention as "a determination to act in a certain way." Attention can lead to knowledge and understanding. Intention leads to action. BP had long paid attention to what was going right and what

---

1 Heath, C. and Heath, D. (2010). *Switch: How to Change Things When Change Is Hard*. Broadway Books, New York, NY

was going wrong. However, only when they became intentional were they able to shift their strategy and achieve exponential success.

Sir Ken Robinson, author of the best-selling book, *The Element,*[2] and an internationally recognized leader in the development of creativity, innovation, and human potential, describes the difference between imagination and creativity. He explains, "Creativity is a step beyond imagination because it requires that you actually do something rather than lie around thinking about it. It's a very practical process of trying to make something original." Intention is about turning what we know and want into something tangible by taking effective action.

Conflict, Intention, and the Compassion Triangle

We have suggested that the purpose of conflict is to create. We have also demonstrated how conflict in the drama triangle is a destructive, competitive, win-lose proposition. In this context, intention can become extremely damaging. Conflict within drama is a powerful force that draws people in, creates strong agendas, alienates, polarizes, and encourages intention towards unhealthy goals. Examples of persons who were highly successful at advancing their agendas using intention in the drama triangle include Adolf Hitler and Osama Bin Laden.

Intention from within the compassion triangle is life-giving and transformative. Conflict from within the compassion triangle allows for the creative process of transcending while including. While this process is by no means easy, the long-term benefits can be astonishing: think Mahatma Gandhi and Mother Theresa.

So, when conflict is present, carefully examine your process. Are you entering drama? Are you sensing the unfolding of a win-lose scenario? Are you exhibiting characteristics of the persecutor, rescuer, or victim? If so, intention will manifest as self-justification and will not turn out

---

2 Ken Robinson with Lou Aronica (2009). *The Element. How Finding Your Passion Changes Everything.* Penguin Books, London.

well. Make sure you are in the compassion triangle before setting your intention.

How can you harness the power of intention? Here are five elements that will help you move toward success.

Five Keys to Intention Within the Compassion Triangle

Measure It

It's well known that what gets measured, gets worked on. If turnover is something you want to improve, then measure it. If higher sales is a goal of yours, then measure sales indicators. If on-time deliveries are something you want, track them. If losing weight is what you want, weigh yourself regularly. Without clear indicators of where you are, you can't plot a course toward success. While measuring and tracking your goals is critical for intention, it is not sufficient for success. Rarely is information, data, and even knowledge sufficient for positive change.

Want It

To make intention work you must drop expectations, focus on what you want and be determined to get it! When you become intentional about this process, failure becomes a stepping stone to success. When you expect it rather than want it, failure becomes an excuse for disappointment and backsliding. Getting clear about what you want, what you truly want, means peeling back the layers of expectations you have put on yourself or that others have placed on you. If you are doing it to please someone else, dig deeper. If you are doing it because it's your duty, dig deeper. Unless and until you want it, keep digging.

Focus on What's Working

Contrary to traditional industrial, linear, left-brained logic, trying to improve a process by focusing on what's broken is not particularly effective. In fact, it often leads to drama. From manufacturing, to education, to mental health treatment, more and more evidence supports the formula, *focus on what you want more of.* British Petroleum wanted more fruitful wells, so they focused on the wells most likely to be fruitful; they wasted no energy trying to figure out why the poor wells were that way. If you want to reduce turnover, study the people and departments with lowest turnover. If you want to increase sales, look to companies who are excelling. If you want to know how to lose weight and keep it off, talk to people who have done it.

Paradoxically, focusing on what's not working can often worsen the problem. One reason is that it's a negative approach and can set up win-lose, drama-based interactions. Focusing on what's not working tills fertile soil for persecutor, victim, and rescuer behavior. This, in turn, plants the seeds of self-justification, excuses, and reliance on quick fixes.

I (Nate) experienced a powerful example of this with a manufacturing client of ours. We were working with their production team on improving communication, teamwork, and cohesiveness. They were fully interdependent on the production line, each relying on the other for the process to go smoothly. Prior to one of our weekly group coaching visits, I learned that one of the men on the line (we'll call him "David") had dropped a tool into the conveyor, literally putting a wrench in the gears. After three hours and $30,000 of lost productivity, the conveyor was fixed. When David arrived at our meeting, his head was down, he avoided eye contact, and he sat in an out-of-the-way place where he wouldn't have to interact with anyone. Clearly in the victim role, I wondered how his teammates would respond.

Sometimes our clients surprise us! David's two strongest motivators were recognition of person and sensory stimulation. We knew this because he had received his personality communication profile when we trained the team in the Process Communication Model. One by one, David's teammates came over to him. One put a hand on his shoulder and said, "I know how tough this is. I did this once and I felt horrible." Another co-worker said, "Hey, man, you're OK. We're here for you." As the supportive comments flowed, David's head came up. His confidence visibly grew and he began participating in the conversation.

Guess what never happened? A root-cause analysis. There was no conversation about what had gone wrong, about David's competence, about the flow of work on the production line, or how this could have happened and how to prevent it in the future. Everybody knew the answer. David was a longtime productive employee. He was an incredible asset to the team. When his positive motivational needs were met, the problem was solved. David's team focused on the positive.

As an alternative to expectations and enforced standards, imagine making an intentional goal to replace expectations with wants and then focusing on what's working. For instance, in a meeting with your managers or supervisors, you express that you want a five percent decrease in staff turnover. Then ask your supervisors and managers to focus on how they have kept the current staff that they have. See what happens. Watch the innovation percolate.

Respond Instead of Reacting

Another critical element in intentionality is being responsive instead of reactive. When I react, I behave automatically, without care or intention. I often make impulsive, pressured or poorly uniformed decisions. Reactive decisions are like reflexes. When our body responds reflexively, the signals are processed at the level of the spinal cord, not the brain, which means that no thinking, judgment or evaluation take place. While the old saying "Any decision is better than no decision" still holds true, a responsive decision is a responsible decision.

Responding requires presence of mind, perspective, self-awareness, and a sense of one's environment. Responsibility is the ability to respond; i.e.being Response-Able. Response-able leaders pair experience with new learning and practice to give them a repertoire of options from which to choose. They never say things like, "I had no choice," or "You left me no option." They are response-able because they know they always have choices and aren't afraid to own them or to learn new ways of being more effective. They face challenges with confidence because they have learned to turn mistakes into stepping stones for success.

In the compassion triangle we are able to respond openly, resourcefully, and persistently. In the drama triangle we react automatically and irresponsibly, based on old habits of thinking and relating. For this reason, responding is much more difficult and takes more energy than reacting. Reacting is easier because we've justified our belief that we aren't or can't be responsible for a different outcome.

Most companies can observe and notice a problem. Successful companies do not focus or make decisions based on that problem. They make responsive decisions based on what they want and what's working. They transcend and include with intention.

Companies and individuals who react instead of responding find themselves frequently putting out fires. This is a byproduct of drama. Micromanaging, overcontrolling, and focusing on what's not working are often the major culprits.

Company A wants change. They invest in a two-year plan to train all employees in the direction that they want to go. They hold all employees accountable to that direction.

Company B expects their employees to meet standards. When problems arise they put those fires out and write stricter policies. When the fires get too hot, they terminate the employee.

Which company do you want to work for? Which company will have lower turnover, higher engagement, and higher performance?

Own and Understand Choice

Being intentional is also about owning and understanding choice. You can choose to make decisions that enable you to drill four out of five and keep you responsive to life conditions. You can choose to be Luke Skywalker instead of Darth Vader. You are responsible for your choices, good or bad. Regardless of what happens, you are making choices constantly. Own your choices and understand that each one comes with a consequence.

When you are intentional, you are going to make mistakes and endure some pain. And, you can fail forward because what you want and who you are has not changed. Those who fail backwards are easily disappointed in themselves or others and lose faith, blame others, or become cynical. Those who own their choices are able to fail forward. They model optimism and inspiration.

I (Nate) can remember living with attention instead of intention. I couldn't begin to tell you everything that was wrong with my job and the world. Nobody appreciated my hard work or great ideas. Everything I tried was met with resistance. I complained that nobody could see the opportunity right in front of their noses. I was a total downer to be around. When I started living with intention, I stopped complaining and started focusing on what I wanted instead of what was wrong. Now, my clients often tell me that enthusiasm and optimism are what they like best about me. I'm often accused of being lucky as well. Since living with intention results in more opportunity, I'm not sure luck has much to do with it.

We end this chapter with a story of a man who changed the world by following the five keys to intention within the compassion cycle;

- Measure it
- Want it
- Focus on what is working
- Be responsive
- Own and understand choice

Barry Marshall was convinced that he had a cure for peptic ulcers in a common, readily available antibiotic. However, existing regulations in the scientific and medical community prevented him from experimenting on humans. Mainstream gastroenterologists of the day did not buy into his theory and held on to the prevailing hypothesis that ulcers were caused by stress.

Marshall had a theory that H. pylori bacteria caused common peptic ulcers. However no one would believe him or let him experiment on people to prove his theory. So, what to do? He found the only human patient that he could experiment on — himself. He cultured and ingested H. pylori from the gut of a sick patient.

After a few days he began to vomit and become extremely exhausted. To test his theory, he took his experimental antibiotic. He cured himself and went on to prove without a doubt that this available antibiotic was an effective treatment for ulcers.

As it turned out, not only did this antibiotic cure ulcers, it also became an effective treatment for stomach cancer. So, by giving himself an ulcer and experimenting on himself, Marshall found a cure for stomach cancer and ulcers, almost completely ridding the world of these two diseases. In 2005 he was awarded the Nobel Prize for Physiology or Medicine. He was able to accomplish this despite the lack of support and barriers put up by the medical community.

Many people look back on their life and say, "I wish I had. ..." Are you one of those people? In order to accomplish what you really want out of life, you may have to take some risks. You also have to listen to yourself and not others, even though the others might be trusted and popular. If Marshall had listened to the status quo, we may not have the cure for ulcers and stomach cancer.

Throughout your life, certain people will tell you what you should do and what is right for you. People will question you, put up barriers, and feel threatened by your enthusiasm. We all have a cure. When you live with intention, you can claim yours — just as Marshall claimed his.

CHAPTER 14

Advocates and Adversaries: Building Healthy Community

Adversaries operate from within the drama triangle and attempt to draw others into drama with them for a win-lose game. Advocates operate from within the compassion triangle, and invite others to join them for win-win outcomes.

During a recent presentation at a state human resource provider conference, a woman shared with me (Nate) a powerful story of the cost of adversarial relationships. Her hospital had researched and selected a vendor to help implement a new electronic medical record system. It was the right system for their needs, the vendor had a great track record, and they had the money to invest.

Three years into the implementation, they abandoned the project. Due to adversarial relationships within the company they were unable to move forward. A key Information Technology manager felt threatened by the project, and rather than being honest, she passive-aggressively undermined progress. Another manager resented having his staff take time away from their regular duties to learn the new system. Rather than dealing with the conflict in a healthy way, he found ways to make it difficult for his staff to get free, thus slowing down their progress.

Their total loss: $13 million, including $8 million for the product and $5 million in lost productivity.

When you have adversaries in your life, you know it. You can feel the drain, animosity, and pressure to watch your back. You know that they want nothing more than for you to suffer, lose, and go down in flames. They get satisfaction in watching you suffer and fail.

You also know what it feels like to have advocates in your life. These people and organizations are looking out for your best interests, going to bat for you, believing in you and celebrating your successes. They are not afraid to be honest with you, and hold you accountable, even when it's hard.

Here's a brief summary of the qualities and behaviors of each. See which of these resonate with your experience:

Advocates	Adversaries
Seek multiple perspectives and offer perspective to others	Become tunnel-visioned and expect limited options from others
In touch with reality	Only in touch with their own distorted reality
Appreciate and utilize diversity	Have prejudices, jump to conclusions, and lead with assumptions
Embrace and facilitate conflict that creates	Sow the seeds of destructive conflict
Seek to be effective	Seek to feel justified
Fail forward, learning from mistakes	Fail backwards, repeating the same mistakes
Seek empowerment in others	Seek power for themselves by trying to control others

Advocates	Adversaries
Look for connections and commonalities	Look for exceptions and focus on differences
Work for something	Work against something
Celebrate others' success	Minimize, feel resentful, or are jealous of others' success
Refuse to take sides	Take sides and create camps
Add energy to systems and relationships	Are energy vampires, sucking the life out of systems and relationships

Table 1: Characteristics of Adversaries and Advocates

Would you prefer advocates or adversaries in your relationships with your co-workers, supervisors, employees, management team, executive team members, family, friends, and other people in your world? Unless you'd like to feel like a martyr or victim all the time, we suspect that most people would prefer advocates to adversaries. Either way, you can take responsibility for these relationships and the choices you've made to get here. You are responsible for the choices you make each day to continue down that path.

If you want to spend more of your energy being an advocate instead of languishing in adversarial relationships, you have some tough choices to make. Let's explore this from a business perspective first, and then look at the personal ramifications.

Adversarial Relationships in Business

How long will you tolerate adversarial relationships at work? How long does someone have to sabotage you, your relationships, and your business before you do something about it? If they are adversaries, their behavior and attitudes are costing you money, morale, time, reputation, and energy.

Many of you have let adversaries do daily or weekly damage in your workplace because you cannot or will not take steps to move out of drama. When we train leaders on the dynamics of distress and drama, not a single session goes by where someone doesn't share a story of allowing an adversary to damage an organization for much too long. Over time, adversarial behavior becomes normative. Systems, processes, policies, and those unwritten rules of the culture support the behavior and make it very difficult for positive change to happen. We make excuses, transfer people to different supervisors and departments, and cover for the damage they cause.

Why do you allow adversaries in your workplace? Most likely, it's because you and your company culture are built around one or more of the four myths. If you believe deep down that someone or something else can control your "OK-ness," or that you can control someone else's "OK-ness," you are behaving according to a myth.

Are you afraid of what will happen if you confront adversarial behavior? That's a natural response and has probably been reinforced by past experience. Is this fear drawing you into drama so that you play the role of victim or rescuer? If so, you are not only compromising your best self, but you are now partly responsible for the problems. Drama is a 50/50 proposition.

Do you respond to adversarial relationships by becoming adversarial yourself and going on the counter-attack? If so, you are playing the role of persecutor. You are not only compromising your best self, you are now 50 percent responsible for the problems in the workplace.

The excuses for staying in drama are endless:

"My boss will take it out on me if I confront the behavior."

"Judy in accounting has a small but loyal following that will revolt if we fire her."
"What will people think?"
"I'll just tough it out until retirement."
"It's not worth the hassle."
"It won't make a difference anyway."
"I can't afford to lose my job over this."

Each of these excuses feels convincing if you have reinforced it through your own behavior for months and years, if you've bought into the myths that support it, and if you've progressively closed off other options. Still, you are responsible for your choices and your situation. We encourage you to write down your concerns, excuses, and fears for continuing in your drama role(s). For each one, what is a compassionate alternative? How might you respond if you practiced openness, resourcefulness, and persistence? This is a first step in owning your choices and entertaining other possibilities.

Adversarial Relationships in Personal Life

Adversarial relationships exist in our personal lives as well with the people we love and care about most.

Do you have a personal relationship that is adversarial and riddled with drama? Do you feel taken advantage of or disappointed? Do you dread spending time with this person, but do it anyway? Does communication frequently break down or end in arguments? Do you feel attacked or disrespected on a regular basis?

What are the consequences? Stress, strained relationships, distractions, depression, divorce, abuse, poor health...the list goes on. You feel trapped, angry, and resentful. Over time you begin to question your own value and the value of others around you. How can you be your best self under these conditions? How can you be productive in work and life when you are perpetually mired in a win-lose relationship?

Why do you tolerate it? Perhaps for the same reasons you tolerate adversaries in the workplace. When people buy into the myths long enough, behavior follows, and habits are formed that keep us from seeing that we are valuable people who can make choices.

You might be thinking, "That's harsh! I know I have choices, but come on, we aren't in control of things and sometimes bad things happen. I have to cope. That's life. If I try to change my situation, there will be serious repercussions."

If you were in the room with me now, I would say, "Absolutely! You are 100 percent right. Thank you for pointing this out. Every choice has a consequence." Let's explore choices and consequences of dealing with adversaries.

Options for Dealing with Adversaries

Do Nothing. Put Up with It.

It is a perfectly legitimate and understandable choice for you to do nothing. You can choose to continue to suffer, continue to complain, feel like a victim, lash out and fight back, be a martyr, or choose whatever habit of survival you've become accustomed to. We're not here to judge you.

The upside of doing nothing is that you don't have to change. You don't have to face the risk and discomfort of not knowing what to do next. You can't fail if you don't try anything new. Life is pretty predictable and it can continue to be that way. And, if you have surrounded yourself with people who will play along with your drama, why upset the apple cart? They might not like or accept you if you stop playing the game.

The downside of this choice is that by doing nothing you are also choosing the consequences. I (Nate) have done a lot of work with victims of domestic violence. These are horrible situations in which the perpetrator has done everything in his power to control, manipulate, remove options, and frighten the victim into staying in the relationship. In most cases, victims of abuse have been manipulated to believe the myths that "You can make me feel good, and you can make me feel bad" over years and years of abuse. Consequently, their options seem to diminish, and their perpetrator does his best to reinforce this assumption by controlling everything from money to time to who the victim associates with.

As we work with victims who are taking charge of their lives, the recurring theme is that they recognize that nothing will change until they change. This realization and the choices that come with it in no way condones the behavior they've tolerated and have no reflection on whether the victim is OK as a person. When the victim can separate choices and behaviors from their OK-ness, forward progress begins. And, along with change comes more consequences — the risk of rejection, pressure to revert to old habits, a host of unknowns, and perhaps most frightening, the risk of success. Sometimes the consequences hurt as much as the pain they are trying to move away from. This is part of the process of change — pain that is chosen, purposeful, and meaningful.

Advocacy requires assertiveness. Instead of doing nothing, the other choices we take require us to set boundaries, protect those boundaries, and initiate healthy relationships with others. When we avoid assertiveness or don't know how to be assertive, there are three typical alternative paths we can take: aggressive, passive, and passive-aggressive. The recipe for an adversarial relationship is to mix and match aggression, passive-aggression, and passivity. Let's take a closer look at these three ingredients.

Aggressive responses reflect the persecutor role in the drama triangle. This involves verbal, physical, and emotional abuse. The aggressive person attacks others to get what they want. They yell, intimidate, bribe, manipulate, blame, and threaten in order to get their way. We have both had bosses who threatened to reduce our salary if we did not comply with their edicts. Needless to say we have never been good at complying through a victim role. Hopefully, neither will you.

Passive responses reflect the victim role in the drama triangle and involve doing nothing and not speaking up for yourself, your peers, or your community. People playing the passive role want others to feel sorry for them, and they spend a significant amount of the time feeling sorry for themselves. They are often seen as pushovers. Persecutors in their community can and will take advantage of them. After making a mistake, people taking the passive option will say things like, "I am just so stupid," "I deserve to be fired," "No one thought I could do a good job any way," "If I stand up to my boss he'll fire me," or "If I let my wife know how I am really feeling, she'll think I am weak."

Passive-aggressive responses are another way to pursue a false sense of power in the drama triangle while doing nothing constructive. The passive-aggressive person can play multiple roles in the drama triangle. They tend to be flippant and sarcastic. They say one thing while their body and tone of voice say another. They talk about others behind their backs, often stirring the pot and causing controversy. They stuff their feelings one day and act like a martyr, and blow up at people the next day, keeping everyone guessing whether Jekyll or Hyde is going to show up. They rarely mean what they say because they're playing both sides of the aisle to advance ulterior drama agendas.

A typical passive-aggressive pattern occurs in companies when employees stay quiet during staff meetings even though they disagree with what's being said. By remaining silent, they implicitly agree with what's being said. Later, they complain about what's going on and attack their superiors in the safety of their cubicles and break rooms. This behavior makes it unsafe for anyone to be assertive during meetings because they fear they'll be left out on a limb without advocates. And, it is unfair to leadership because they don't get accurate feedback about how employees are feeling.

Whether through being aggressive, passive, or passive-aggressive, people who chose any one of these three alternatives to assertiveness are avoiding responsibility for their behavior and the health of their community. It works as long as others play along.

Surround Yourself with Advocates

Think of a time when you were in your best space, both in your business and personal worlds. You were happy, your needs were being met, you dealt with stress well, and life was good. Who was in your world? What types of people did you surround yourself with? Advocates!

To create and support a healthy community, we must have advocates around us. A healthy community is one that recruits and rewards advocates. Compassionate relationships require support. Being open, resourceful, and persistent is difficult, particularly as we begin to challenge drama-based habits and relationships. When we are learning new skills, we benefit from role models, cheerleaders, and others who truly believe in us. Anyone who has tried to make significant personal change knows the value of a support network. This is true in our personal as well as our professional lives.

Surrounding yourself with advocates has consequences. The upside is that you have a lot of positive energy behind you. You have someone to catch you when you fall, hold up a mirror to your drama, and celebrate your successes.

Of course, there are also downsides. If you've been living in drama for a long time, you may have a hard time finding genuine advocates. Don't mistake someone who always agrees with you and always takes your side on issues for an advocate. If they're not willing to hold you accountable for mistakes, they're just allowing you to stay justified and delusional. After all, misery loves company. Try using the list in Table 1 as your selection criteria for advocates. Or, complete our online Drama Assessment at drama.next-element.com, assessing people in your life to see how you experience them on the nine dimensions of drama. It may prove harder than you think. Advocates tend to steer clear of adversaries, and compassion-seekers generally don't spend a lot of time with drama-seekers. So, be prepared for a challenging search.

Another downside of surrounding yourself with advocates is that you may make some enemies. Your existing friends may not take kindly to your new relationships. Most likely, they will feel threatened, jealous, and exposed when you begin spending more time with advocates. It's not surprising that persons recovering from addiction usually have to eliminate old playmates and playgrounds in order to be successful. A key component of recovery is replacing adversaries with advocates.

It is possible to surround yourself with advocates even if you haven't yet made any new choices with the adversaries in your life. In fact, if you are contemplating taking action to change adversarial relationships, we suggest you begin by building your team of advocates first. Find people whom you can lean on, who believe in you, and who will hold you accountable for change before you jump into the ring. Practice with them, play out scenarios, share with them your excuses for staying in drama, do contingency planning. Do whatever it takes for you to build your confidence to change the way you relate to adversaries.

Invite Adversaries into the Compassion Triangle

When you make the choice to stop tolerating adversarial relationships, two options open up. You can either invite adversaries into more healthy interactions, or end the relationship. We investigate these choices in detail in the next chapter.

CHAPTER 15

The Power of Invitation

We've chosen to emphasize invitation because nobody has control over another human being. Invitations are just that. They are not ultimatums. Invitations preserve the integrity of both parties even when unhealthy behavior is occurring. They emphasize that the choices we make are about us and do not impact anyone's "OK-ness." Invitations reject myths and reinforce "I'm OK. You're OK." Invitations send the message that others can make choices as well.

The Formula for Compassionate Conflict

Here is a template we've used with many clients to help them craft an invitation, begin moving out of drama, and entering creative conflict. Its called the Formula for Compassionate Conflict and includes six steps: Identify your feelings, describe problematic behaviors, connect the dots, ask for what you want, stop and listen, and have a follow-through plan.

Let's take a look at each component of this formula. At any time, skip to the end of this section to see real-life examples.

1. Identify Your Emotions (Open)

The first step is to be honest with yourself and the other person about how you feel in this adversarial relationship. As hard as this may be, it is a necessary step toward owning your part in the relationship and respecting the choices of the other person. For some, this may take time, learning, and self-examination to identify the authentic feelings that have been buried beneath the drama. It's OK to take your time, consult your advocates, and get outside help if necessary. There are many terrific self-help resources focused on helping you identify your emotions. When one of the four myths has been guiding your beliefs and behavior, it will take some effort to identify and own your authentic feelings.

When you are ready, complete the first step (below).

I feel _____

2. Describe the Behavior (Open and Resourceful)

What behaviors are you having problems with? What is it that the other person does that is so troublesome for you? Be specific and be clear. You may just not like their attitude or tone. That's pretty vague. When you can be specific about the behaviors associated with the attitude or tone, your invitation will be more effective. For example, "Stand over me with your arms crossed looking down at me." This is a critical step that cannot be skipped. Drama is about acting on assumptions about others, projecting intentions onto their behavior, and seeking self-justified rationales for our own interpretations. Invitations into compassion avoid these temptations. To identify a person's behavior objectively requires careful examination of all of these factors.

The next part of the formula is now waiting for you.

I feel _____
when you _____

3. Connect the Dots (Open and Resourceful)

Explain the connection between your feelings and the other person's behaviors. Why do you feel this way? What is it about the behavior that is uncomfortable for you? When you do this, you must own your unique interpretations, perceptions, experiences, and baggage from the past. There are legitimate reasons why certain behaviors are difficult for you. Your reasons may not apply to everyone. They apply to you. You owe it to yourself and to the other person to be clear about that. Connecting the dots is where you can begin to examine the difference between "responsible to" and "responsible for." You are responsible to yourself for how you interpret, react, and are affected by others' behavior. You are *not* responsible for their behavior. The more you explore, understand, and process this with advocates in your life, the more prepared you'll be to move into compassion.

Now you are ready to fill in the third part of the compassion equation.

I feel _____
when you _____
because _____.

4. Ask For What You Want (Resourceful and Persistent)

What alternative behaviors do you want? What compassionate alternative are you looking for? It's not sufficient to ask someone to just stop doing something you don't like. What behavior do you want instead? Be clear, specific, and respectful.

Your colleague is being a "jerk." Before you confront him, identify what specific behaviors are "jerk-like." Does he insult you in front of peers? Does he dismiss your ideas in a particular way? What about his tone and body language? Words like "mean," "jerk," "pain in the butt," even "disrespectful," are loaded labels and mean different things to different people. To reduce the chance of misunderstanding, assumptions, and defensiveness, be very clear about the observable behaviors you have experienced.

The habitual roles you've previously played on the drama triangle can make this a difficult task. Victims are used to believing that they never get what they want so have stopped trying to figure it out. Persecutors are used to believing that others are incapable of giving them what they want so have come to expect failure from them. Rescuers have convinced themselves that their own answers are the best so have stopped asking permission to help others. The victim must make the transition to believing that they are worthy of having needs, desires, and getting what they want. Persecutors must make the transition to recognizing that others are capable, competent, trustworthy, and that their own behaviors have prevented others from giving them what they want. Rescuers must make the transition into allowing solutions and answers other than their own and recognizing that everyone is OK regardless of whose solution it was.

When we facilitate this step with teams, we are astounded by how often the outcome of this step is effective beyond what anyone believed possible, and also how difficult and frightening it is. When people drop the prejudices, assumptions, and projections that accompany their drama role and simply ask for what they want, it's amazing how well this is often received by the other person. Responses such as "Wow, I never knew this bothered you so much," "I am so grateful to know this," and "So what I've been trying is not having the intended result. I am so sorry" are not uncommon.

To begin asking for what you want requires you to examine and challenge three core beliefs that you've probably clutched onto in the Drama Triangle.

Do I deserve to get what I want? If you've come to believe that you don't deserve to be happy, fulfilled, or respected, it may be difficult to authentically ask for what you want. If you've become accustomed to the self-fulfilling prophecy of failure, it will be challenging to believe that it can happen for you. Many times people are unsuccessful at asking for what they want, not because they don't say the words, but because they don't believe it down deep. Consequently, their behaviors send them right back into the victim role. They sabotage their own efforts. How would you respond to this statement: "You'll probably hate this idea, but..." What a setup! Sounds like the person saying it already expects that the idea will be rejected. Instead, the individual could simply ask, "Will you listen to my idea?"

Can others contribute to my happiness? Have you decided that people can't be trusted? Have you closed yourself up so as never to be let down or betrayed again? If so, it will be very difficult to ask others for what you want. You may say the words, but the rest of your body language — pursed lips, rigid posture, lack of eye contact — will say that you don't believe it will happen. As a result, you've just invited the other person to feel unsafe, untrusted, or attacked. They will likely respond in a guarded or defensive way, thus reinforcing your belief. What's the result? You get just what you expected: they failed you once again. To make the change, you must rekindle your belief in others — in their capacity, potential, and desire to be advocates. Give them a real chance. If you start a sentence with "I don't expect you to understand, but..." you are setting the other person up to be defensive, and setting yourself up to be disappointed by their response. Instead, try asking, "Will you share with me your understanding of this?"

What will happen if I believe and act differently? "What if" may be the most powerful question in human history. It has the power to open up amazing possibility (in compassion), and the potential to create fear, stop forward progress as well as lock us down in analysis paralysis, invite us to question ourselves, lose confidence, and lead us into the pits of drama. Some common "what if" questions include:

> *"What if it doesn't work?"*
> *"What if I fail again?"*
> *"What if I succeed and then people expect things of me?"*
> *"What if really bad things happen that we didn't even anticipate?"*

The power of "what if" is that it taps into our capacity to imagine realities that have not yet happened. Only human beings can do this. We are self-reflective, capable beings who want not only to control our present lives, but our futures as well. The downside is that by asking this question, we transport ourselves into a place where we have no control and our minds can highjack our emotions and psyche. We have allowed ourselves to be sucked into the false belief that the outcome can somehow define us and our essential OK-ness. Imagine the freedom you'd have to try new things if you truly believed that while your choices have consequences that you are responsible for, your OK-ness is never at stake. That belief is what led Marshall to his discovery.

We offer the following five affirmations to help you transcend the negative pull of "what if."

- It hasn't happened yet and you have no control over it.
- Whatever your fear may be; it's not as likely to happen as you anticipate.

One or two significant experiences have you paralyzed. You've been ruled by the fear that it could happen rather than actual experience.[1] Consequently, you've avoided testing your theory countless times in the past which only reinforces that you are justified in your fear.

- You only have this moment. All you can control is what you do next.
- There will be consequences even though you don't know what they are yet. And, you are capable of handling them.
- You are OK even if you fail, don't get what you want, or don't know all the answers.

As you accept, embrace, and start practicing these five truths about "what if" you will become able to complete the next part of the formula and ask for what you want.

I feel _____
when you _____
because _____.
I would prefer _____.

5. Stop and Listen (Open)

OK. You've said your piece. Now it's time to stop, listen, and learn. By asking, "What is your perspective?," you are letting the other person know you are open-minded and willing to listen. You are giving the individual a chance to respond and feel heard as well. This is a great way to reduce defensiveness. When I (Nate) assign clients and students to practice this formula, largely half of them report never

---

1 In the Greek legend of The Sword of Damocles, the value of the sword hanging above Damocles was not that it fell, but that it hung. There can be nothing happy for the person over whom some fear always looms.

getting past this step. The other person is grateful for the feedback and spontaneously offers positive change.

To practice this step, read through what you've written so far, and finish by asking, *"What's your perspective?"*

Then take five deep breaths.

6. Follow Through (Resourceful and Persistent)

Because you are only inviting, you cannot control what the other person does about your request. The person could very possibly ignore you, reject your offer, argue and disagree with your reasons, disregard your feelings, or be indifferent. None of these are in your control. The other person's response does not define your OK-ness and in no way alters the validity of your request. You are in control of all the work you've done in the first five steps of this formula and how you've gotten to this point. You are in control of your non-negotiable boundaries and how you will respond to maintain your dignity and stay out of drama.

Your follow-through plan is all about your taking responsibility for pursuing what you want. Consequently, your plan must include what you are willing to do to get it, or what you're willing to do if you don't get it in order to preserve your dignity and boundaries. It may involve creative consequences, incentives, or any manner of attempts to positively influence those around you from within the compassion triangle. It will also include your plan B in the event that you don't get the behavior you want. The best plans are open, resourceful and persistent. In all cases, the follow-up plan maintains an "I'm OK. You're OK" attitude, regardless of the outcome.

Right about now, it's very common for supervisors, parents, and others in authority roles to challenge this formula with the belief that it's impossible to impose consequences on someone from within the compassion triangle. Subordinates challenge us about the "what ifs" of enforcing consequences with superiors.

We want to remind readers that this is not a "hug a thug" model. This is not about letting people off the hook. It's about wanting from within the compassion triangle. It's about being effective. Without a follow-through plan, your invitation means nothing and is likely to be disregarded by adversaries because they realize you don't really mean business and are not willing to advocate for yourself.

Consequences can be enforced compassionately. You may explain that if you don't get what you are asking for, there will be consequences. You can articulate this from within the compassion triangle in an open, resourceful, and persistent way without attacking, over-adapting, or beating around the bush.

Your plan may include how you will take care of yourself even if the other person doesn't honor your request. It may mean leaving a relationship, quitting a job, or otherwise refusing to be around a person who is caught in drama. Regardless, your plan is your plan and will require persistence to follow through.

Are you are ready for the fifth step in the formula?

I feel _____
when you _____
because _____ .
I would prefer _____ .
What's your perspective?
I am prepared to _____ .

We recommend you write out your formula, refine it, and rehearse it with an advocate before delivering it to your adversary. Many of our clients journal for days or even weeks before actually confronting the difficult person in their lives. It's OK to take your time. And, it's OK to start small with conflict that seems manageable to you. With practice it will become easier and you will learn better ways to do it.

Examples of the Formula for Compassionate Conflict

Professional

"I feel disrespected when you check your computer during staff meetings because my time is important and I am giving my undivided attention to the team. I would prefer that you close your computer during meetings. What's your perspective? I am prepared to remind you of this in the future before jumping to conclusions or becoming frustrated."

"I feel unmotivated and depersonalized when you compliment my work every day because although I am a hard worker, I am also a person. I would prefer that you ask me about my family and let me socialize a bit more at work. What's your perspective? I am prepared to be accountable to our performance standards and to be reminded about what I need in order to do my best work as often as you want."

"I feel disrespected when you don't share pertinent information with me that I need in order to do my job because I am held back from doing my best work and being proactive with our customers. I would prefer that we touch base regularly and you share more information with me. What's your perspective? I am prepared to request a job transfer if I continue to feel held back."

Personal / Family

> *"I feel embarrassed and anxious when you kick me and demand candy in the checkout line at the grocery store because I am stuck in line and people are watching. I would prefer that you ask me nicely for what you want and then accept my answer. What's your perspective? I am prepared to go straight to the car next time this happens, even if it means we don't have groceries for dinner."*

> *"I feel afraid when you aren't home at your curfew because the later it gets, the more drunk drivers there are on the road. I would prefer that you let me know where you are and be home before 11:00 p.m. What's your perspective? I am prepared to take away your cell phone and ground you as an incentive to help motivate you."*

> *"I feel angry when you tease me in front of our friends and family because it sets a bad example for our children. I would prefer that you say positive things in public, and if you have problems with my behavior that we deal with it privately. What's your perspective? I am prepared to confront you or leave a party to maintain my dignity."*

Inviting Adversaries Out of Your Life

Sometimes, one of you has to go. There may come a point where you have tried all the other options and things have not changed. This is when it's time for one of the most difficult decisions of all — the decision that someone has to go. And sometimes that person is you.

This is not about winners and losers. It's not about admitting defeat or delivering the final blow. It's about taking ownership of your well-being. It's about being self-ful. We'll delve further into this topic in the next chapter.

When we chose to leave our last employer, it was tough. Making this difficult choice involved the dissolution of healthy, as well as unhealthy relationships. We were unable to grow our circle of advocates within this particular company, so we left. Complaining, attacking, blaming, and feeling victimized didn't change anything. We chose to move away from adversaries, surround ourselves with new advocates, and own both the positive and negative consequences of those choices.

On a personal level, I (Jeff) have chosen to end relationships with certain individuals and family members because they were adversaries. While these were difficult and painful decisions, I needed to make them. I wanted to be healthy and knew that these relationships were bringing me down. I chose to do what was best for me, my circle of advocates, and my community.

Sometimes, other people have to go. In professional settings, this means terminating someone if you have the authority to do so. It means saying, "Enough is enough." And, you can do this from within the compassion triangle. If the behavior continues, if it is damaging to productivity and morale, and if you've tried invitations, then make the compassionate call and terminate the relationship. Don't blame. Don't persecute. Don't play the victim role. You don't have to beat yourself up; you don't have to beat him up. Just tell him it's time to go.

Maybe you went against your better judgment as a supervisor and hired the wrong person. Admit it, learn from it, and move on. Don't keep digging a hole trying to fix it to save face. Maybe you are afraid of ramifications from the drama camps in the organization. That's OK. They are OK and you are OK. Move forward and deal with the consequences openly, resourcefully and persistently.

In numerous situations we've helped an employer or supervisor terminate someone who refuses to stay out of drama and refuses invitations into compassion. On many occasions we hear later that both parties are better off. Each one needed to take that step, make the necessary choices, and grow. The same is true for personal relationships. If you find yourself repeatedly sucked into drama in personal relationships, it's time to let go.

Letting go doesn't happen without pain or consequences. When it's time to end a relationship, there can be grief, loss, anger, unfinished business, regrets, and a host of other emotions to deal with. For help with letting go, a great place to start is with the work of Melody Beattie.[2]

As you move on to the next chapter on being self-ful, ask yourself, *"Do I want a community of advocates or adversaries? Do I want advocates or adversaries working in my company?"* Either way, you have the power to create it and take full responsibility for the choice you make. As the Jedi Knight Yoda said, "Do or do not. There is no try". Translation: There is the drama world of adversaries and the compassion world of advocates. Choose wisely.

---

2 Beattie, M. (1990). *The Language of Letting Go: Daily Meditations On Codependency. Hazeldon*, Center City, MN

CHAPTER 16

Becoming Self-Ful

"In the unlikely event of a loss of cabin pressure, an oxygen mask will automatically appear in front of you. To start the flow of oxygen, pull the mask towards you. Place it firmly over your nose and mouth, secure the elastic band behind your head, and breathe normally. Although the bag does not inflate, oxygen is flowing to the mask. If you are travelling with a child or someone who requires assistance, secure your own mask on first, and then assist the other person."

—Announcement during pre-flight safety demonstration

Meet Cheryl, a mother of three whose primary job is to keep the home running. The choice was hers and she is supported by her husband. She gets up before her children every morning to get ready for the day. She makes breakfast, gets lunches ready, makes sure kids are dressed appropriately, and is on the road to drop them off at several different schools. After the drop-offs, Cheryl comes home, cleans up the breakfast mess, does laundry, cleans the house, and starts the prep work for dinner. She may be able to fit in a women's group meeting, a trip to the grocery store, and pay some bills. Then, she gathers up her kids' uniforms, equipment, and supplies. She picks them up from school, takes one to soccer, one to ballet, and the other to the library. An hour later, she picks up the kids and takes them home for a snack.

Before long it's dinner time, and Cheryl serves a tasty, balanced meal for her family. After dinner she helps the kids finish their homework, completes forms for school pictures, and makes sure that showers and bedtime routines are taken care off. She gets all three kids to bed before cleaning up the kitchen, paying some more bills, and going through the mail. By 10:00 p.m. she is tired, overwhelmed, and ready to crash. She collapses into bed, worries about her children and reminisces about a childhood family vacation for a few minutes before falling asleep.

Tomorrow she does it all over again.

Meet Cheryl's husband, Roger, whose primary job is to make the money to keep the home running. He made this choice with his wife's support. He wakes at 6:00 a.m. to read the paper, watch the business news, and prep for his day at work. The market is tough and being out of a job is not an option. After he packs his briefcase and gets dressed, he grabs a bagel, blows kisses to Cheryl and the kids, and is out the door. Once at work the words *won't* and *no* are not in his vocabulary, and his peers and supervisors know it. He works through lunch, goes to meetings that were not on his agenda, and takes on one of his co-worker's projects that was falling behind. He takes a breath, looks down at his watch and sees that it's 7:30 p.m. After a 30-minute commute, he's home just in time to say good night to his children as they drift off to sleep. He goes into the kitchen, heats up his dinner plate and takes it to the living room where he watches TV, eats, and falls asleep. Around midnight he wakes up, takes his plate to the kitchen, and heads to bed to find his wife fast asleep. He's in for about five hours of sleep.

Tomorrow, he does it all over again.

One evening, Roger comes home from work to a strangely silent house. There is a note on the kitchen table. "I've taken the kids to live with my mother for a while," the note reads in Cheryl's familiar handwriting. "You were never here for us."

This is a tragedy of selfishness. Neither Cheryl nor Roger took care of themselves and their needs, instead giving priority to the needs of their family, household obligations and job. Both were equally caught up in the belief that one should do for others before taking care of oneself. Ironically, the resentment, illness, and fatigue that developed led to burnout, despair, and a fractured family.

Please don't get caught up into the content of the story. It's not about a job, a family, or ballet lessons. The story is about the hazards of putting others first. By neglecting their own needs, wants and boundaries, Roger and Cheryl became selfish.

Usually, we think of selfishness as the human tendency to be self-serving. Rejecting this tendency completely and abandoning self is just as harmful as becoming egocentric and indulgent at the expense of others. Putting others first and hoping they appreciate your selflessness is selfish. Sidelining your own needs in the service of others is drama because you are believing the myth that you can make others feel good emotionally if you develop the perfect student, ballet dancer, soccer player, or baked chicken casserole. Maybe you are working 70 hours a week and taking over others' work because you believe the myth that others can make you feel bad emotionally if you aren't perfect, work harder than anyone else, or impress your boss with what you've accomplished. This is drama.

As we know, drama encourages you to begin having expectations of yourself and others. You may say to your daughter, "I expect you to be home by eleven." You may say to your employee, "I expect you to have this project completed to perfection." Next, you start to compete, trying to be a better mom than the moms you see in your community, attempting to be a better dad than your dad was to you, striving to be a better provider than you father or mother, charging ahead to outperform all other employees or to be the best manager, CEO or president the company has ever had.

To be selfish is to put others first for unhealthy reasons, to be in the drama triangle, hold expectations, and to compete with a win-lose mindset.

The healthy alternative to this is to be "self-ful." This word is neither in the dictionary nor even in Wikipedia at this writing. We define *self-ful* as attending first to your own health and needs so that you have the energy to be the best mom, dad, husband, wife, employee, CEO, or executive that you can possibly be. The art of being self-ful is to live in the compassion triangle while establishing appropriate boundaries and saying no to drama.

Selfish individuals worry that, "If I say no, what will people think of me?" "If I go home at 5:00 p.m., if I don't volunteer for that new social committee or if I tell my boss that I will start working only 45 hours a week instead of 60, bad things will happen and I might not be OK."

When I am self-ful, I am not worried about what people think about me. I know that my OK-ness is not dependent on either my actions or what others say. I make decisions that are best for me, so that I can go out and make a significant and meaningful contribution in the world. When I am self-ful, I am in tune with myself. I know when I am tired and I rest. I know when I need help and I ask for it.

In his book, *Deep Survival: Who Lives, Who Dies, and Why?*,[1] author Laurence Gonzales shares stories and research demonstrating that children lost in the woods survive at much higher rates than adults. The reason: When they are tired they sleep; when they are hungry they eat; when they are thirsty they drink. Because they are self-ful and listen to their bodies, they are more likely to survive. Adults push on too long, get dehydrated, over-exert, become confused, misuse their resources, and are over reliant on their support equipment (e.g. compass, map) at the expense of common sense. Because they behave selfishly rather than self-fully, they are more likely to die.

Many adults have taught themselves not to listen to their bodies. Is it self-ful to rely on antacids to compensate for eating too much fatty food, drinking too much alcohol and caffeine, and allowing yourself to become overstressed? Is it self-ful to use stimulants and energy drinks to compensate for lack of sleep? Children don't do these things until we teach them to. While children are often accused of being selfish, we may want to examine their keen ability to get their fundamental needs met. It is something many adults have forgotten along the way.

Being self-ful can be a challenging process, and it is a highly worthwhile one. It requires that you operate from within the compassion triangle because your behavior will likely create some conflict between you and others and within yourself. It will require that you challenge long-held myths about yourself and others; to transcend old beliefs and include wisdom you've gained along the way. It will require you to have advocates to assist and support you. Finally, it will require you to embrace the consequences of your choices.

---

1 Gonzales, L. (2003). *Deep Survival: Who Lives, Who Dies, and Why?* W.W. Norton, New York, NY.

CHAPTER 17

Living Beyond Drama:
Transcending Energy Vampires

The focus of this book is on the process skills to be effective in personal and professional relationships. We want to leave you with a step-by-step guide for maximizing the tools in this book to live beyond drama and spend more time in the compassion triangle. The result: You will be happier, more productive, and enjoy more fulfilling relationships at work and at home. These steps outline a trajectory you can implement, starting today.

Step 1: Accept Awareness

The first step in moving beyond drama is to be aware of who you are. What are your natural tendencies, triggers, and behaviors in drama? How are you motivated? What do you do to get negative attention? What gifts and strengths and confidences do you possess that prepare you to be open, resourceful, and persistent? In what areas do you want to grow?

It's also vital to be aware of others. Are you able and willing to recognize drama coming at you? What behaviors, triggers, and tendencies in others are you able to detect? How do these fit with your own drama behaviors? What gifts in others might be useful assets in helping you spend more time in compassion? Who could be your advocates?

Step 2: Accept Imperfection

Of course, no one can stay in the compassion triangle all the time. The inspiration trajectory is a journey of gradually increasing self-awareness and practice failing forward. Accepting imperfection is the key to keeping hope and optimism alive. Knowing in advance that you'll make mistakes along the way will help you to accept them and move on. Trying to avoid imperfection or letting it take you down are all about drama. Embracing imperfection is your doorway into compassion.

Step 3: Accept Choice

You don't have a choice about everything in life. You didn't choose your parents, or the weather, or the political and economic conditions in which you live. You certainly can't choose how other people will respond to you. What you can choose and continue to choose every day are your responses, and what you do next. Regardless of what happens, you can choose compassion at anytime. There will surely be consequences. And, when you accept choice you can own these consequences.

Step 4: Accept Being Self-Ful

Tuning, fueling, and maintaining your engine is the core to living compassionately. Without it you can't think clearly, be available to others, or spend the energy needed to transcend the energy vampires in your life. This is easier said than done, and we've offered many perspectives and methods to tackle the barriers within you that keep you from being self-ful. Know how to get your needs met and do it consistently. Work through all the baggage that has gotten in your way.

Step 5: Accept Response-Ability

Responsibility is the ability to respond, not react. Reacting requires no skill or self-control. It is an impulse that's executed preconsciously and automatically. All too often, reacting gets us into drama because it initiates the habitual routines that we've practiced thousands of times before. Same old tune, different verse.

Response-ability builds on each of the previous four steps; awareness of yourself and others, ownership of your choices, accepting the imperfection that comes with learning and growing, and taking care of yourself. Response-ability improves as you gain confidence in your OK-ness and your skills to live openly, resourcefully, and persistently in all areas of your life.

By taking ownership of your life, you can begin transcending your energy vampires, begin living beyond drama, and help to create a better world for yourself and for all those around you.

NOTES

NOTES

ABOUT THE AUTHORS

Nate Regier, PhD

As the son of Mennonite missionary parents, Nate spent most of his childhood in Zaire and Botswana. Growing up in Africa kindled his optimistic view of human nature and passion for creative problemsolving. Following undergraduate studies at Bethel College in Newton, Kansas, Nate completed his PhD in clinical psychology from the University of Kansas with emphases in clinical counseling, neuropsychology, and behavioral research. Nate worked for 11 years as a clinical psychologist in a community mental health setting where he gained experience in addictions treatment, neuropsychological assessment, and group therapy. He helped launch an integrated behavioral medicine clinic within a multi-specialty medical center where he began to develop his skills in consulting, coaching, and training.

Seeds were planted for the next chapter of his life when Nate discovered outdoor experiential learning through a local ropes course. This ignited his passion for alternative learning methods, moving beyond the therapy room, and exploring the nuances of group dynamics. In 2005 Nate took over leadership of the organizational consulting division where he was working and knew he'd found his calling.

In 2008 Nate joined his coauthor Jeff and two other partners to form Next Element Consulting. He hasn't slowed down since! Nate is in his element when he can bring together his rich background in the social sciences, a hunger for new learning, and a natural passion for creating outstanding client experiences. For Nate, no two days are the same. He relishes a diverse mix of training, advising and coaching, mentoring new employees, business development, product development, outcomes research, and imagining new ways to help delight clients. He travels across the United States and internationally, delivering keynote addresses, training, advising, and coaching.

Nate lives in Newton with his wife, Julie, and their three daughters, Asha, Emily, and Lauren. When he's not attending one of his children's sports or school events, he loves woodworking, tennis, and cooking. Nate is a member of a competition barbeque team and is on the eternal quest for the holy grail of buffalo hot wings. Active in his local community, Nate enjoys facilitating more effective group functioning and volunteers his services on various boards, committees, and community organizations.

Jeff King, MSW

Jeff grew up in Greensburg Kansas and went on to get a bachelor's degree in sociology from Emporia State University and masters degree in social work from Newman University. Jeff has been the director of a residential treatment facility for boys, a psychotherapist specializing in addiction, a ropes course facilitator, and a business owner. In October of 2008 Jeff joined his coauthor Nate and two other partners to found Next Element Consulting. While with Next Element Jeff consulted in the business and educational world, guiding such entities to have better engagement, alignment, and leadership environments.

Jeff is the son of retired teachers and it is no coincidence that in January of 2012 he became the Head of School at the MUSE school in Calabasas, California.

Jeff, his wife, and three kids all live in Calabasas. Jeff's passion is to teach individuals how to live a passionate life and to do what they love. Jeff helped design the MUSE School Learning Plan, which is a specific and progressive way to engage students to learn. This Learning Plan includes two of Jeff's other passions, the Process Communication Model and Self Efficacy. Jeff finds his sweet spot when he is teaching individuals of all ages how to communicate better and to be efficacious.